D1308787

CLASSIC
MAIN COURSES

Classic
Main Courses

OVER 75 RECIPES FOR MARVELOUS MAIN MEALS

CONSULTANT EDITOR
Linda Fraser

ANNESS
PUBLISHING

© Anness Publishing Limited 1995

All rights reserved. No part of this publication may be reproduced,
stored in a retrieval system, or transmitted in any way or by any means, electronic,
mechanical, photocopying, recording or otherwise, without
the prior written permission of the copyright holder.

ISBN 0–8317–1491–3

Editorial Director: Joanna Lorenz
Project Editor: Linda Fraser
Designers: Tony Paine and Roy Prescott
Photographers: Steve Baxter, Karl Adamson and Amanda Heywood
Food for Photography: Wendy Lee, Jane Stevenson and Elizabeth Wolf Cohen
Props Stylists: Blake Minton and Kirsty Rawlings
Additional recipes: Carla Capalbo and Laura Washburn

Printed and bound in Singapore

 The apple symbol indicates a low fat, low cholesterol recipe.

CONTENTS

Introduction *6*

Light Lunches *12*

Mid-week Suppers *30*

Roasts, Pies and Hot-pots *54*

Dinner Party Dishes *72*

Index *96*

PREPARING MEAT FOR COOKING

Whether quickly broiled or stir-fried, or long-simmered for a rich flavor, meat lends itself to endless variety. Here, we give you the preparation tips and techniques that make meat cooking simplicity itself. Although you can buy meat ready for cooking from butchers and supermarkets, some cuts need further preparation, depending on how they are to be cooked.

HOW MUCH TO BUY

As a general guide, when buying boneless meat that has little or no fat, allow 5–7oz per serving. For meat with bone that has a little fat at the edge, allow about 8oz per serving. Very bony cuts such as shin and spareribs have proportionally little meat so you will need 450g 1lb per serving.

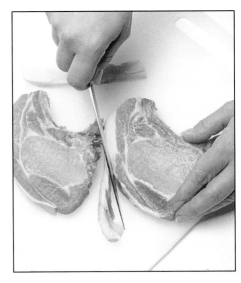

1 **To trim**: use a sharp knife to trim skin or rind and fat from the surface. Leave a little fat on steaks to be broiled, and slash this fat at regular intervals to prevent the steak curling up during cooking. Roasts should retain a thin layer of fat about ⅛–¼in. Cut away the sinew and tough connective tissue.

2 If you like, cut and scrape all fat and gristle from the ends of protruding bones (such as on chops or roasts that contain rib bones). Cover the bone ends with foil to prevent charring.

3 **To chine a roast**: for large cuts of meat that contain rib bones, such as beef rib roast, pork loin and rack of lamb, it is a good idea to cut the chine bone (backbone) where it is joined to the rib bones, to loosen it or to remove it completely before cooking. Do this with a meat saw and sharp knife or ask your butcher to do it. Without the chine bone, the joint will be easy to carve.

4 **To bard a roast**: if a very lean piece of meat is to be roasted without a protective crust (a spice mixture, oil and crumbs or pastry, for example), it is a good idea to bard it to keep it moist. Wrap very thin slices of beef fat, pork fatback or blanched bacon around the roast and tie them in place. Discard the fat before serving but keep the bacon, if liked.

5 **To tie a boned roast**: cuts that have been boned should be tied into a neat shape for roasting or pot roasting. The butcher will do this, but if you want to add a stuffing or seasoning, you will need to retie the joint yourself. Reshape it into a neat roll that is even in circumference. Use butcher's string to make ties around the circumference of the joint at 1in intervals.

GRINDING MEAT

Ground meats of all kinds are easily obtainable, but when you want something more unusual for a pâté or you want to use a particular cut of meat, well trimmed of gristle and tendons, you will grind it yourself. Also, if ground meat is to be served raw, as in steak tartare, it must be freshly prepared.

1 **With a grinder**: this produces the most uniform ground meat, and you can choose coarse or fine grinds, according to which blade is used. Trim the meat well and cut it into 1¼ in cubes or strips, then feed through the machine.

2 **With a food processor**: trim the meat carefully (be sure to remove all gristle because a food processor will chop gristle too) and cut it into cubes. Place in the machine fitted with the metal blade and pulse.

3 In between turning the machine on and off a few times, stir the meat around so that it is evenly ground. Care must be taken not to overprocess meat to a paste, particularly if making hamburgers.

4 **By hand**: trim the meat well. Using a large chef's knife, first cut the meat into cubes, then chop into smaller and smaller cubes. Continue chopping until you have the consistency you want, coarse or fine.

PREPARING MEAT SCALLOPS

Scallops, or scaloppine are slices of veal top or bottom round, cut ⅜ in thick. They need to be pounded before cooking, to break the fibers. This tenderizes them and helps to keep them flat during cooking. Slices of other meat or poultry may also be prepared in the same way as veal, such as turkey cutlets or beef slices, cut from the round, to be rolled and braised.

POUNDING IT OUT

You can also use the base of a heavy saucepan or frying pan to pound and flatten meat scallops. Choose a pan with a smooth base.

1 Trim any fat and gristle from around the edge of each scallop. Lay it flat between two sheets of plastic wrap or wax paper.

2 Using the smooth side of a meat pounder or the long side of a rolling pin, pound gently but firmly all over the scallop to flatten it to ⅛–¼ in thickness. It will spread out to almost twice its original size.

ROASTING MEAT

The dry heat of oven-roasting is best suited to tender cuts of meat. If they don't have a natural marbling of fat, bard them. Alternatively, marinate the meat or baste it frequently with the roasting juices during cooking.

Meat should be at room temperature for roasting. Roast on a rack in a pan that is just a little larger than the joint.

There are two methods of roasting meat. For the first, the joint is seared at a high temperature and then the heat is reduced for the remainder of the cooking time. For the second method, the joint is roasted at a constant temperature throughout.

SUGGESTED ROASTING TIMES

Following the second roasting method, in a 180°C oven, approximate timings in minutes per 1lb:
   Beef, rare, 20 + 20 extra
       medium, 25 + 25 extra
       well done, 30 + 30 extra
   Veal, 25 + 25 extra
   Lamb, 25 + 25 extra
   Pork, 35 + 35 extra
(*Prime cuts such as rib of beef and tenderloin need less time.)

1 According to the recipe, rub the roast with oil or butter and season. If wished, for extra flavor, with the tip of a sharp knife make little slits in the meat all over the surface. Insert flavorings such as herbs, slivers of garlic, olive slices.

2 Roast for the suggested time, basting if necessary. Transfer the cooked meat to a carving board. Leave it to rest for 10–15 minutes before carving. During this time, make a gravy with the roasting juices, if liked.

MEAT THERMOMETER READINGS			
Beef		**Lamb**	
rare	125–130°F	rare	130–135°F
medium-rare	135°F	medium	140–145°F
medium	140–145°F	well done	160°F
well done	160°F		
		Pork	
Veal		medium	150°F
well done	160°F	well done	160–165°F

TESTING FOR DONENESS

The cooking times given in a recipe are intended to be a guideline. The shape of a cut can affect how long it takes to cook, so testing is essential.

NATURAL LAW OF ROASTING

A joint will continue to cook in its own retained heat for 5–10 minutes after being removed from oven or pot, so it is a good idea to take it out when it is just below the desired thermometer reading.

1 Large roasts can be tested with a metal skewer. Insert the skewer into the thickest part and leave it for 30 seconds. Withdraw the skewer and feel it: if it is warm, the meat is rare; if it is hot, the meat is well cooked.

2 The most reliable test is with the use of a meat thermometer, inserted in the center of the joint, away from bones. Follow manufacturer's instructions. See the chart for the internal temperatures.

DEGLAZING FOR A PAN SAUCE

After pan-frying or sautéing, a simple yet delicious sauce can be made in the pan. The same method can be used to make gravy for roast meats. It is also a good way to maximize flavor in stews and casseroles.

Before deglazing, remove the meat and keep it warm. Pour or spoon off all the fat from the pan, unless the recipe calls for shallots, garlic, etc. to be softened. In that case, leave 1–2tsp of fat and cook the vegetables in it.

1 Pour in the liquid (wine, stock, vinegar, etc). Bring to a boil, stirring well to scrape up all the browned bits from the bottom of the pan.

2 Boil over high heat for 1–2 minutes or until the liquid is almost syrupy. Add cream or butter if you like, then season to taste and serve.

MAKING GRAVY

Gravy made from the roasting juices is rich in flavor and color. It is a traditional accompaniment for roast meat and poultry.

> ## RESTING A JOINT BEFORE CARVING
>
> Once a joint is removed from the oven or pot, it should be left in a warm place to 'rest' for 10–15 minutes. During this time, the temperature of the joint evens out, and the flesh reabsorbs most of the juices.

1 Spoon off most of the fat from the roasting tin. Set the tin over moderately high heat, add flour and stir to combine well.

2 Cook, scraping tin well until it forms a smooth brown paste. Add stock or liquid and bring to a boil, stirring. Simmer, then season.

SEARING MEAT FOR POT-ROASTING OR ROASTING

Meat is sometimes seared as the first step in its cooking. This may be done either by roasting briefly at a high temperature and then reducing the heat or by frying. The result is a browned crust that adds delicious flavor.

> ## POT-ROASTING OR BRAISING
>
> This method of cooking tenderizes even the toughest cuts of meat.
>
> Depending on the desired result, meat to be pot-roasted may or may not have an initial searing.

1 **To sear by frying**: dry the meat well. Heat a little oil in a frying pan or flameproof casserole until very hot. Fry meat over high heat until well browned. Turn the meat using two spatulas or spoons.

2 If roasting, transfer the meat to the oven. If pot-roasting, add a small amount of liquid and cover the casserole tightly. If a frying pan has been used for searing, be sure to deglaze it (see above).

STIR-FRYING

The preparation of ingredients for stir-frying often takes longer than the cooking itself. This is because all ingredients must be cut to uniform sizes so that the cooking can be accomplished quickly and evenly.

A wok is excellent for stir-frying because its high sides let you stir and toss the ingredients briskly. Use long cooking chopsticks or a wooden spatula to keep the ingredients moving around the wok.

1 Prepare all the ingredients in uniformly sized pieces following recipe instructions.

2 Heat a wok or large deep frying pan over medium-high heat. Dribble in the oil down the sides.

3 When the oil is hot (a piece of vegetable should sizzle on contact), add the ingredients in the order specified in the recipe. (Those that take longer to cook are added first.) Do not add too much to the wok at a time or the ingredients will start to steam rather than fry.

4 Fry, stirring and tossing constantly with chopsticks or a spatula, until the ingredients are just cooked: vegetables should be crisp-tender and meat and poultry tender and juicy.

5 Push the ingredients to the side of the wok or remove them. Pour liquid or sauce as specified in the recipe into the bottom. Cook and stir, then mix in the ingredients from the side. Serve immediately.

PAN-FRYING AND SAUTÉING

Tender cuts of meat, such as steaks and chops, slices of calves' liver and hamburgers, are ideal for cooking quickly in a heavy frying pan. And the juices left in the pan can be turned into an easy sauce.

Before pan-frying and sautéing, trim excess fat from steaks, chops, scallops, etc., then dry them very thoroughly with paper towels.

For cooking, use a fat that can be heated to a high temperature. If using butter, an equal amount of vegetable oil will help prevent burning.

1 Heat the fat in the pan over high heat until very hot but not browning. Put in the meat, in one layer. Do not crowd the pan.

2 Fry until browned on both sides and done to your taste. If pan-frying pork or veal chops, reduce the heat to moderate once they are in the pan.

MAKING MEAT STOCK

The most delicious meat soups, stews, casseroles, gravies and sauces rely on a good home-made stock for success. Neither a stock cube nor a canned consommé will do if you want the best flavour. Once made, meat stock can be kept in the refrigerator for four or five days, or frozen for longer storage (up to six months).

ON THE LIGHT SIDE

For a light meat stock, use veal bones and do not roast the bones or vegetables. Put in the pot with cold water and cook as described.

Makes about 2 quarts

4lb beef, veal or lamb bones, such as shank, knuckle, leg, and neck, cut into 2½in pieces
2 onions, unpeeled, quartered
2 carrots, roughly chopped
2 celery stalks, with leaves if possible, roughly chopped
2 tomatoes, coarsely chopped
4½ quarts cold water
a handful of parsley stems
a few fresh thyme sprigs or ¾tsp dried thyme
2 bay leaves
10 black peppercorns, lightly crushed

1 Preheat the oven to 450°F. Put the bones in a roasting pan or flameproof casserole and roast, turning occasionally, for 30 minutes or until they start to brown.

2 Add the onions, carrots, celery and tomatoes and baste with the fat in the tin. Roast for a further 20–30 minutes or until the bones are well browned. Stir and baste occasionally.

3 Transfer the bones and vegetables to a stockpot. Spoon off the fat from the roasting pan.

4 Add a little of the water to the roasting pan or casserole and bring to the boil on top of the stove, stirring well to scrape up any browned bits. Pour this liquid into the stockpot.

5 Add the remaining water. Bring just to a boil, skimming frequently to remove all the foam from the surface. Add the parsley, thyme, bay leaves and peppercorns.

6 Partly cover the pot and simmer the stock for 4–6 hours. The bones and vegetables should always be covered with liquid, so top up with a little boiling water from time to time if necessary.

7 Strain the stock through a strainer. Skim as much fat as possible from the surface. If possible, cool the stock and then chill it; the fat will rise to the top and set in a layer that can be removed easily.

LIGHT LUNCHES

In the middle of the day meals need to be quick to prepare
and eat. In this chapter there are plenty of speedy, yet delicious,
recipes to choose from. There are rice dishes, noodles with
shrimp, tasty home-made burgers, a vegetarian bake made
with chick-peas and artichokes, and several very simple, yet
filling, pasta dishes to tempt you. Try Tagliatelle with Hazelnut
Pesto; if you use fresh pasta, it will be ready to serve in
well under 10 minutes.

Kedgeree

Popular for breakfast in England in Victorian times, Kedgeree has its origins in *Khichri*, an Indian rice and lentil dish, and is often flavored with curry powder.

INGREDIENTS

Serves 4

1¼lb smoked haddock
½ cup long grain rice
2 tbsp lemon juice
⅔ cup light or sour cream
pinch of freshly grated nutmeg
pinch of cayenne pepper
2 hard-boiled eggs, peeled and cut
    into wedges
4 tbsp butter, diced
2 tbsp chopped fresh parsley
salt and black pepper
parsley sprigs, to garnish

1 Poach the haddock, just covered by water, for about 10 minutes, until the flesh flakes easily. Lift the fish from the cooking liquid using a slotted spoon, then remove any skin and bones flake the flesh.

2 Pour the rice into a measuring cup and note the volume, then tip out, pour the fish cooking liquid into the cup and top up with water, until it measures twice the volume of the rice.

3 Bring the fish cooking liquid to a boil, add the rice, stir, then cover and simmer for about 15 minutes, until the rice is tender and the liquid absorbed. While the rice is cooking, preheat the oven to 350°F, and butter a baking dish.

4 Remove the rice from the heat and stir in the lemon juice, cream, flaked fish, nutmeg and cayenne. Add the egg wedges to the rice mixture and stir in gently.

5 Tip the rice mixture into the baking dish, dot with butter and bake for about 25 minutes.

6 Stir the chopped parsley into the Kedgeree, check the seasoning and garnish with parsley sprigs.

COOK'S TIP

Taste the Kedgeree before you add salt, since the smoked haddock may already be quite salty.

Noodles with Shrimp in Lemon Sauce

As in many Chinese dishes the fish is here purely for color and a little flavor. You could serve this as an accompaniment with several others, or as part of a Chinese-style meal.

INGREDIENTS

Serves 4

2 packages Chinese egg
  noodles
1 tbsp sunflower oil
2 stalks celery, cut into
  matchsticks
2 garlic cloves, crushed
4 scallions, sliced
2 carrots, cut into matchsticks
3in piece cucumber, cut into
  matchsticks
4oz shrimp in shells
1 lemon, or 2 tbsp lemon sauce
1 tsp cornstarch
4–5 tbsp fish stock
1 cup shelled shrimp
salt and black pepper
few sprigs dill, to garnish

1 Put the noodles in boiling water and leave to soak as directed on the package. Meanwhile, heat the oil in a pan and stir-fry the celery, garlic, scallions and carrots for 2–3 minutes.

2 Add the cucumber and whole shrimp and cook for 2–3 minutes. Meanwhile, peel the rind from the lemon and cut into long thin shreds. Place in boiling water for 1 minute.

3 Blend the lemon juice, or lemon sauce, with the cornstarch and stock and add to the pan. Bring gently to a boil, stirring, and cook for 1 minute.

4 Stir in the shelled shrimp, the drained lemon rind and seasoning to taste. Drain the noodles and serve with the shrimp, garnished with dill.

— COOK'S TIP —

These noodles can also be deep-fried. Once cooked as above, drain on kitchen paper. Deep-fry small amounts at a time, until golden brown and very crisp.

Pasta Carbonara

An Italian favorite and a classic Roman dish, whose name translates as 'charcoal burners' pasta'. Traditionally made with spaghetti, it is equally delicious with fresh egg tagliatelle.

INGREDIENTS

Serves 4

12oz–1lb fresh tagliatelle
1 tbsp olive oil
8oz piece of ham, bacon or pancetta,
   cut into 1in sticks
4oz (about 10) button mushrooms,
   thinly sliced
4 eggs, lightly beaten
5 tbsp light cream
2 tbsp finely grated Parmesan cheese
salt and black pepper
fresh basil sprigs, to garnish

1 Cook the pasta in a pot of boiling salted water, with a little oil added, for 3–4 minutes or until al dente.

2 Meanwhile, heat the oil in a frying pan and add the ham, bacon or pancetta. Fry for 3–4 minutes, add the mushrooms and fry for a further 3–4 minutes. Turn off the heat and reserve. Lightly beat the eggs and cream together in a bowl and season well.

3 Drain the cooked pasta and return it to the pan. Add the ham, bacon or pancetta, the mushrooms and any pan juices and stir into the pasta.

4 Pour in the eggs and cream and half the Parmesan cheese. Stir well and as you do this the eggs will cook in the heat of the pasta. Pile on to warmed serving plates, sprinkle with the remaining Parmesan and garnish with basil.

Baked Macaroni and Cheese

A classic American supper - replace the Cheddar with your family's favorite cheese.

INGREDIENTS

Serves 4

1 tbsp olive oil
2⅓ cups short cut macaroni
2 leeks, chopped
4 tbsp butter
½ cup flour
3¾ cups milk
2 cups grated sharp Cheddar cheese
2 tbsp ricotta cheese
1 tsp whole grain mustard
1 cup fresh bread crumbs
½ cup grated Double Gloucester
   cheese
salt and black pepper
1 tbsp chopped fresh parsley,
   to garnish

1 Preheat the oven to 350°F. Bring a large pot of salted water to a boil and pour in the olive oil. Add the macaroni and leeks and boil gently for 10 minutes. Drain, rinse under cold water and reserve.

2 Heat the butter in a saucepan, stir in the flour and cook for about a minute. Remove from the heat and gradually add the milk, stirring well after each addition until smooth. Return to the heat and stir continuously until thickened.

3 Add the Cheddar cheese, ricotta cheese and mustard, mix well, and season with salt and pepper.

4 Stir the drained macaroni and leeks into the cheese sauce and pile into a greased ovenproof dish. Level the top with the back of a spoon and sprinkle over the bread crumbs and Double Gloucester cheese.

5 Bake for 35–40 minutes. Serve hot, garnished with fresh parsley.

Pork and Celery Popovers

Lower in fat than they look, and a good way to make the meat go further, these little popovers will be popular with children.

INGREDIENTS 🍎

Serves 4
sunflower oil, for brushing
1¼ cup flour
1 egg white
1 cup skim milk
½ cup water
12oz lean ground pork
2 celery stalks, finely chopped
3 tbsp oatmeal
2 tbsp snipped fresh chives
1 tbsp Worcestershire sauce
salt and black pepper

1 Preheat the oven to 425°F. Brush 12 deep muffin pans with a small amount of oil.

2 Place the flour in a bowl and make a well in the center. Add the egg white and milk and gradually beat in the flour. Gradually add the water, beating until smooth and bubbly.

3 Place the ground pork, celery, oatmeal, chives, Worcestershire sauce, and seasoning in a bowl and mix well. Mold the mixture into 12 small balls and place in the muffin pans.

4 Cook for 10 minutes, remove from the oven, and quickly pour the batter into the pans. Cook for 20–25 minutes more, or until puffed and golden brown. Serve hot with thin gravy and fresh vegetables.

COOK'S TIP

Transfer the batter to a jug so that you can easily and quickly divide it among the patty pans, then return to the oven at once – the pan must not be allowed to cool down or the popovers won't rise.

Cornish Pasties

These individual pies from Cornwall in England were the original packed lunch. In the past cooks added whatever ingredients were available.

INGREDIENTS

Makes 6

1¼–1½lb ready-made pie pastry
1lb chuck steak, diced
1 potato, about 6oz, diced
6oz rutabaga, diced
1 onion, chopped
½ tsp dried mixed herbs
a little beaten egg, to glaze
salt and black pepper

1 Preheat the oven to 425°F. Divide the pastry into six equal pieces, then roll out each piece of pastry to an 8in round.

2 Mix together the steak, vegetables, herbs and seasoning, then spoon an equal amount on to one half of each pastry round.

--- COOK'S TIP ---

Other vegetables, such as turnip, carrot or celery could be used in place of the rutabaga, if you prefer.

3 Brush the pastry edges with water, then fold the free half of each round over the filling. Press the edges firmly together to seal.

4 Use a metal spatula to transfer the pasties to a cookie sheet, then brush each one with beaten egg.

5 Bake the pasties for 15 minutes, then reduce the oven temperature to 325°F and bake for a further hour. Serve hot or cold.

Cauliflower Cheese

INGREDIENTS

Serves 4

1 cauliflower, broken into large florets
3 tbsp butter
1 small onion, chopped
2 slices lean bacon, chopped
3 tbsp flour
scant 2 cups milk
1 cup grated sharp Cheddar cheese
pinch of mustard powder
salt and black pepper

1 Cook the cauliflower in boiling salted water until almost tender. Drain well and tip into a baking dish.

2 Meanwhile, melt the butter in a saucepan and gently cook the onion and bacon until the onion is soft, then spoon over the cauliflower.

3 Stir the flour into the butter in the pan and cook, stirring, for 1 minute. Remove the pan from the heat and slowly pour the milk into the pan, stirring all the time.

4 Return the saucepan to the heat and bring to the boil, stirring constantly. Simmer for 4–5 minutes, stirring occasionally.

5 Preheat the broiler. Remove the pan from the heat and then stir in three-quarters of the cheese. Add the mustard and seasoning to taste.

6 Pour the cheese sauce over the cauliflower, then sprinkle the remaining cheese over the top and put under the broiler until the top is golden and bubbling.

Golden Cheese Pudding

INGREDIENTS

Serves 4

2½ cups milk
1¾ cups fresh bread crumbs
1½ cups grated sharp Cheddar cheese
1½ tsp Dijon mustard
4 eggs, separated
salt and black pepper

1 Bring the milk to the boil, then stir in the bread crumbs and remove from the heat. Beat in the cheese, mustard and egg yolks.

2 Season the bread crumb mixture, then set aside for 30 minutes.

3 Meanwhile, preheat the oven to 350°F and butter a shallow 6¼ cup baking dish.

4 Whisk the egg whites in a large bowl until stiff but not dry, then carefully fold the egg whites into the bread crumb mixture using a large spoon or a spatula in three batches.

5 Transfer the mixture to the baking dish and bake for about 30–45 minutes, depending on the depth of the dish, until just lightly set and golden.

Toad in the Hole

Sausages are cooked in a light batter which rises to a crisp, brown crust, making this a tasty and substantial supper dish.

INGREDIENTS

Serves 4
scant 1 cup flour
2 tbsp chopped fresh parsley
2 tsp chopped fresh thyme
1 egg, beaten
1¼ cups milk and water, mixed
4 tbsp oil
1lb good-quality sausages
salt

1 Stir the flour, chopped herbs and salt together in a bowl and form a well in the center.

2 Pour the egg into the well, then gradually pour in the milk and water while stirring the dry ingredients into the liquids. Beat to form a smooth batter, then leave for 30 minutes.

3 Preheat the oven to 425°F. Pour the oil into a small roasting pan or baking dish, add the sausages, turn them to coat them thoroughly in the oil, then cook the sausages in the oven for 10–15 minutes, until they are beginning to brown all over and the oil is very hot.

4 Stir the batter using a wooden spoon, then remove the roasting pan or baking dish from the oven and quickly pour the batter over the sausages and return the roasting pan or baking dish to the oven to bake for about 40 minutes (depending on the depth of the batter), until well risen and crisp around the edges.

COOK'S TIP

It is important to preheat the oil with the sausages so that the batter rises well and becomes crisp.

Beef and Mushroom Burgers

It's worth making your own burgers to cut down on fat – in these the meat is extended with mushrooms for extra fiber.

INGREDIENTS

Serves 4

1 small onion, chopped
2 cups small cup mushrooms
1lb lean ground beef
1 cup fresh whole-wheat bread
   crumbs
1 tsp dried mixed herbs
1 tbsp tomato paste
flour, for shaping
salt and black pepper

1 Place the onion and mushrooms in a food processor and process until finely chopped. Add the beef, bread crumbs, herbs, tomato paste and seasonings. Process for a few seconds, until the mixture binds together but still has some texture.

2 Divide the mixture into 8–10 pieces, then press into burger shapes using lightly floured hands.

3 Cook the burgers in a non-stick skillet, or under a hot broiler for 12-15 minutes, turning once, until evenly cooked. Serve with relish and lettuce, in burger buns or pita bread.

COOK'S TIP

The mixture is soft, so handle carefully nd use a fish slice for turning to prevent the burgers from breaking during cooking.

VARIATION

To make Lamb and Mushroom Burgers, substitute lean ground lamb for the ground beef.

Bacon and Egg Bread Pudding

Bacon and egg is such an obvious combination, but perhaps not often thought of as a bread pudding. But it is delicious and could use up leftover ingredients.

INGREDIENTS

Serves 4

8 rashers bacon, crisply broiled, rinded and chopped
5–6 slices bread, buttered
2 eggs
1¼ cups milk
1 garlic clove, crushed
½ cup grated Cheddar cheese
salt and black pepper

1 Sandwich the bacon between the bread slices, cut into triangles and arrange in a buttered ovenproof dish.

2 Mix the eggs, milk and garlic, and season to taste. Pour this mixture over the bread and leave to soak up for about 10 minutes. Meanwhile, preheat the oven to 350°F.

3 Sprinkle the grated cheese over the top of the bread pudding and bake for 30–40 minutes, until golden brown. (Finish off under the broiler if it needs further browning.)

Chick-peas and Artichokes au Gratin

For last-minute extras this is a very quick, extremely tasty, and unusual dish.

INGREDIENTS

Serves 4

14oz can chick-peas, drained
14oz can black-eyed peas, drained
4½oz jar marinated artichokes (or canned artichoke hearts, chopped, plus a little olive oil)
1 red bell spepper, seeded and chopped
1 garlic clove, crushed
1 tbsp chopped fresh parsley
1 tsp lemon juice
⅔ cup sour cream
1 egg yolk
½ cup grated cheese
salt and black pepper

1 Preheat the oven to 350°F. Mix the chick-peas, black-eyed peas, marinated artichokes or artichoke hearts, and bell pepper together.

2 Stir in as much of the artichoke dressing, or oil if using artichoke hearts, as is necessary to moisten the mixture. Stir in the garlic, parsley, lemon juice and seasoning to taste.

3 Mix together the sour cream, egg yolk, cheese and seasoning. Spoon evenly over the vegetables and bake for 25–30 minutes, or until the top is golden brown.

Corned Beef and Egg Hash

This classic American hash is made with corned beef and is a popular brunch or lunchtime dish all over the United States. Serve with chili sauce for a really authentic touch.

INGREDIENTS

Serves 4

2 tbsp vegetable oil
2 tbsp butter
1 onion, finely chopped
1 green bell pepper, seeded and diced
2 large boiled potatoes, diced
12oz can corned beef, cubed
¼ tsp grated nutmeg
¼ tsp paprika
4 eggs
salt and black pepper
chopped fresh parsley, to garnish
sweet chili sauce or tomato sauce,
    to serve

1 Heat the oil and butter together in a large frying pan and add the onion. Fry for 5–6 minutes, until softened.

2 In a bowl, mix together the pepper, potatoes, corned beef, nutmeg and paprika and season well. Add to the pan and toss gently to distribute the cooked onion. Press down lightly and fry on a medium heat for about 3–4 minutes, until a golden brown crust has formed on the bottom.

3 Stir the mixture through to distribute the crust, then repeat the frying twice, until the mixture is well browned.

4 Make four wells in the hash and crack an egg into each one. Cover and cook gently for about 4–5 minutes, until the egg whites are just set.

5 Sprinkle with chopped parsley and cut the hash into quarters. Serve hot with sweet chili sauce.

— COOK'S TIP —

Put the can of corned beef into the fridge to chill for about half an hour before using – it will firm up and cut into cubes more easily.

Beef Strips with Orange and Ginger

Stir-frying is one of the best ways to cook with the minimum of fat. It's also one of the quickest ways to cook, but you do need to choose tender meat.

INGREDIENTS 🍎

Serves 4

1lb lean beef rump, fillet, or sirloin, cut into thin strips
finely grated rind and juice of 1 orange
1 tbsp light soy sauce
1 tsp cornstarch
1in piece ginger root, finely chopped
2 tsp sesame oil
1 large carrot, cut into thin strips
2 scallions, thinly sliced

1 Place the beef strips in a bowl and sprinkle over the orange rind and juice. If possible, leave to marinate for at least 30 minutes.

2 Drain the liquid from the meat and set aside, then mix the meat with the soy sauce, cornstarch, and ginger.

COOK'S TIP

If you haven't any sesame oil, then use sunflower oil, or try flavored chili oil, or a nut oil such as hazelnut or walnut instead.

3 Heat the oil in a wok or large frying pan and add the beef. Stir-fry for 1 minute until lightly colored, then add the carrot and stir-fry for 2–3 minutes more.

4 Stir in the scallions and reserved liquid, then cook, stirring, until boiling and thickened. Serve hot with rice noodles or plain boiled rice.

Tagliatelle with Hazelnut Pesto

Hazelnuts are lower in fat than other nuts, which makes them useful for this reduced-fat alternative to pesto sauce.

INGREDIENTS 🍎

Serves 4

2 garlic cloves, crushed
1 cup fresh basil leaves
¼ cup hazelnuts
⅞ cup skim milk soft cheese
8oz dried tagliatelle, or 1lb fresh
salt and black pepper

1 Place the garlic, basil, hazelnuts, and cheese in a food processor or blender and process to a thick paste.

2 Cook the tagliatelle in lightly salted boiling water until just tender, then drain well.

3 Spoon the sauce into the hot pasta, tossing until melted. Sprinkle with pepper and serve hot.

COOK'S TIP

Italian ricotta cheese makes a good alternative to skim milk soft cheese in this recipe.

Spaghetti with Tuna Sauce

A speedy mid-week meal, which can also be made with other fresh or dried pasta shapes.

INGREDIENTS 🍎

Serves 4

8oz dried spaghetti, or 1lb fresh
1 garlic clove, crushed
14oz can chopped tomatoes
15oz can tuna in water, drained and flaked
½ tsp chili sauce (optional)
4 pitted ripe olives, chopped
salt and black pepper

1 Cook the spaghetti in lightly salted boiling water for 12 minutes or until just tender. Drain well and keep hot.

2 Add the garlic and tomatoes to the saucepan and bring to a boil. Simmer, uncovered, for 2–3 minutes.

3 Add the tuna, chili sauce, if using, olives, and spaghetti. Heat well, add the seasoning, and serve hot.

COOK'S TIP

If fresh tuna is available, use 1lb, cut into small chunks, and add after step 2. Simmer for 6–8 minutes, then add the chili sauce, olives, and pasta.

VARIATION

To make a less hot, herby version of this dish, omit the chili sauce and add 4 tbsp chopped mixed fresh herbs instead.

MID-WEEK SUPPERS

When you are cooking for a family, week-day meals need to be filling fare. Recipes that are a complete main course in one dish, such as Ground Beef with Garlic Potatoes, or Mushroom and Bacon Risotto, are ideal. If you haven't much time on the day for cooking, there are quick recipes that will appeal to children and adults alike: try Bacon Koftas, or make a warming pot of Sausages and Beans with Dumplings.

Rich Beef Casserole

INGREDIENTS

Serves 4–6

2lb chuck steak, cut into cubes
2 onions, coarsely chopped
1 bouquet garni
6 black peppercorns
1 tbsp red wine vinegar
1 bottle full-bodied red wine
3–4 tbsp olive oil
3 celery stalks, thickly sliced
½ cup flour
1¼ cups beef stock
2 tbsp tomato paste
2 garlic cloves, crushed
6oz cremini mushrooms,
    halved
14oz can artichoke hearts, drained
    and halved
chopped fresh parsley and thyme,
    to garnish
creamy mashed potatoes, to serve

1 Place the meat in a bowl. Add the onions, bouquet garni, peppercorns, vinegar and wine. Stir well, cover and leave to marinate overnight.

2 The next day, preheat the oven to 325°F. Strain the meat, reserving the marinade. Pat the meat dry with paper towels.

3 Heat the oil in a large flameproof casserole and fry the meat and onions in batches, adding a little more oil, if necessary. Remove and set aside.

4 Add the celery to the casserole and fry until lightly browned. Remove and set aside with the meat and onions.

5 Sprinkle the flour into the casserole and cook for 1 minute. Gradually add the reserved marinade and the stock, and bring to a boil, stirring. Return the meat, onions and celery to the casserole, then stir in the tomato paste and crushed garlic.

6 Cover the casserole and cook in the oven for about 2¼ hours. Stir in the mushrooms and artichokes, cover again and cook for a further 15 minutes, until the meat is tender. Garnish with chopped parsley and thyme, and serve hot with creamy mashed potatoes.

Liver and Onions

Calves' liver is wonderfully tender and makes this simple dish mouthwateringly delicious. However it is expensive so substitute thinly sliced lamb's liver, if you prefer and cook over a low heat until just tender.

INGREDIENTS

Serves 4
4 tbsp oil
3 large onions, total weight about
  1lb 6oz, sliced
1lb calves' liver, cut into
  ¼in thick slices
salt and black pepper
sage leaves, to garnish

1 Heat 3 tbsp of the oil in a large, heavy frying pan. Add the onions and a little seasoning, cover and cook over a low heat, stirring occasionally, for 25–30 minutes, until the onions are soft.

2 Uncover the pan, increase the heat to medium-high and cook the onions, stirring, for 5–7 minutes until golden. Using a slotted spoon, transfer to a bowl, leaving the oil in the pan.

3 Add the remaining oil to the pan and increase the heat to high. Working in batches so the liver is in a single layer, cook for 45–60 seconds a side until just browned on the outside, and pink inside and tender. Season, then transfer to a warm plate and keep warm while frying the remaining liver in the same way.

4 Return all the liver and the onions to the pan and cook over a high heat for 30–60 seconds. Serve at once, garnished with sage.

--- COOK'S TIP ---

The onions need to be covered during their initial cooking, if your frying pan does not have a lid, use foil as a cover.

Lamb Steaks with Mint Dressing

INGREDIENTS

Serves 4

4 shoulder steaks of lamb
1 large garlic clove, crushed
½ in piece of ginger root, grated
10–12 coriander seeds, crushed
⅔ cup plain yogurt
2 tbsp olive oil
1 tsp walnut or sesame oil
1 tbsp orange juice
2 tbsp chopped fresh mint
½ green bell pepper, seeded and
    finely shredded
1 small red onion, thinly sliced
½ head oak leaf lettuce, torn into
    small pieces
salt and black pepper

1 Place the steaks on a flat dish or tray. Pound together, or crush, the garlic, ginger and coriander seeds, then mix in half the yogurt and seasoning. Spread over the meat and leave for 1–2 hours, turning once.

2 Remove the steaks and scrape off the marinade. Wipe the steaks dry and then brush with a little olive oil and sprinkle with seasoning. Grill or barbecue until as pink, or as well done as you wish.

3 Whisk the remaining olive oil and the walnut or sesame oil into the remaining yogurt with the orange juice, mint, and seasoning to taste. Add a little water if it is too thick for your taste. Toss the pepper, onion and lettuce together lightly.

4 Serve the grilled steaks at once with the tossed salad and the yogurt and mint dressing.

— COOK'S TIP —

Lamb shoulder steaks are the best value for this dish, but not always available – you could use leg steaks or chops instead.

Sausages and Beans with Dumplings

Sausages needn't be totally banned on a low fat diet, but choose them carefully. If you are unable to find a reduced-fat variety, choose turkey sausages instead, and always drain off any fat during cooking.

INGREDIENTS

Serves 4

1lb half-fat sausages
1 medium onion, thinly sliced
1 green bell pepper, seeded and diced
1 small red chili, sliced, or ½ tsp chili
    sauce
14oz can chopped tomatoes
1 cup beef stock
15oz can red kidney beans, drained
salt and black pepper

For the dumplings

2½ cups flour
2 tsp baking powder
1 cup cottage cheese

1 Cook the sausages without fat in a nonstick pan until brown. Add the onion and pepper. Stir in the chili, tomatoes, and stock; bring to a boil.

— COOK'S TIP —

To make a speedy, spicy (though not low fat) version of this recipe, use chorizo sausages or kabanos in place of the half-fat sausages. Cut in thick slices and add to the sauce in step 2.

2 Cover and simmer gently for 15–20 minutes, then add the beans and bring to a boil.

3 To make the dumplings, sift the flour and baking powder together and add enough water to mix to a firm dough. Roll out thinly and stamp out 16–18 rounds using a 3in cutter.

4 Place a small spoonful of cottage cheese on each round and bring the edges of the dough together, pinching to enclose. Arrange the dumplings over the sausages in the pan, cover the pan, and simmer for 10–12 minutes, until the dumplings are puffed. Serve hot.

Ragoût of Veal

If you are looking for a low calorie dish to treat yourself – or some guests – then this is perfect, and quick, too.

INGREDIENTS

Serves 4
1lb veal fillet or loin
2 tbsp olive oil
10–12 pearl onions, kept whole
1 yellow bell pepper, seeded and cut in eight
1 orange or red bell pepper, seeded and cut in eight
3 plum tomatoes, peeled and quartered
4 sprigs of fresh basil
2 tbsp dry martini or sherry
salt and black pepper

1 Trim off any fat and cut the veal into cubes. Heat the oil in a frying pan and gently stir-fry the veal and onions until browned.

2 After a couple of minutes add the peppers and tomatoes. Continue stir-frying for another 4–5 minutes.

3 Add half the basil leaves, coarsely chopped (keep some for garnish), the martini or sherry, and seasoning. Cook, stirring frequently, for another 10 minutes, or until the meat is tender.

4 Sprinkle with the remaining basil leaves and serve hot.

Lamb's Liver with Peppers

If you really want to make a splash for a special occasion, then use sliced calves' liver instead of the lamb's.

INGREDIENTS

Serves 4
2 tbsp olive oil
2 shallots, sliced
1lb lamb's liver, cut in thin strips
1 garlic clove, crushed
2 tsp green peppercorns, crushed (or more to taste)
½ red bell pepper, seeded and cut in strips
½ orange or yellow bell pepper, seeded and cut in strips
2 tbsp crème fraîche or sour cream
salt and black pepper
rice or noodles, to serve

1 Heat the oil and fry the shallots briskly for 1 minute. Add the liver, garlic, peppercorns and peppers, then stir-fry for 3–4 minutes, or until no pink runs from the liver.

2 Stir in the crème fraîche or cream, season to taste and serve at once with noodles or rice.

—— COOK'S TIP ——

Lamb's liver is best when still very slightly pink in the middle, although many prefer it well cooked. With this recipe you could please everyone, but do watch closely as it soon overcooks.

Mushroom and Bacon Risotto

INGREDIENTS

Serves 4

2 tbsp sunflower oil
1 large onion, chopped
3oz smoked bacon, chopped
12oz Arborio or risotto rice
1–2 garlic cloves, crushed
¼ cup dried sliced mushrooms, soaked
in a little boiling water
6oz mixed fresh mushrooms
5 cups hot stock
few sprigs of oregano or thyme
1 tbsp butter
little dry white wine
3 tbsp peeled, chopped tomato
8–10 black olives, pitted and quartered
salt and black pepper
sprigs of thyme, to garnish

1 Heat the oil in a large, heavy-based pan with a lid. Gently cook the onion and bacon until the onion is tender and the bacon fat has run out.

2 Stir in the rice and garlic and cook over a high heat for 2–3 minutes, until the rice is well coated. Add the dried mushrooms and their liquid, the fresh mushrooms and half the stock, the oregano and seasoning. Bring gently to a boil, then reduce the heat to minimum. Cover tightly and leave to cook.

3 Check the liquid in the risotto occasionally by very gently stirring. If quite dry, slowly add more liquid. (Don't stir too often, as this lets the steam and flavor out.) Add more liquid as required until the rice is cooked, but not mushy.

4 Just before serving, stir in the butter, white wine, tomatoes and olives and check the seasoning. Serve hot, garnished with thyme sprigs.

Ground Beef Pie with Garlic Potatoes

This is almost a complete meal in itself, but you could add lots more vegetables to the meat to make it go further.

INGREDIENTS

Serves 4

1lb lean ground beef
1 onion, chopped
3 carrots, sliced
4 tomatoes, peeled and chopped
1¼ cups beef stock
1 tsp cornstarch
1 tbsp chopped, mixed herbs,
    or 1 tsp dried
2 tbsp olive oil
2 garlic cloves, crushed
1¼lb potatoes (3 large), par-cooked
    and sliced
salt and black pepper

1 Preheat the oven to 350°F. Stir-fry the meat and onion in a large pan until browned. Add the carrots and tomatoes to the pan.

2 Stir in the stock, with the cornstarch blended in, and the herbs. Bring to a boil and simmer for 2–3 minutes, then season to taste. Transfer to a shallow ovenproof dish.

3 Mix the oil, garlic and seasoning together. Layer the potatoes on top of the meat mixture, brushing liberally with the garlic oil. Cook for 30–40 minutes, until the potatoes are tender and golden. Serve with a green salad and crisp green beans or snow peas.

---- COOK'S TIP ----

Leave the potatoes unpeeled, if you prefer, in this recipe, and incorporate other par-cooked root vegetables such as carrot, celeriac, rutabaga or turnip, and layer them with the potatoes.

Greek Lamb Pie

INGREDIENTS

Serves 4

sunflower oil, for brushing
1lb lean ground lamb
1 medium onion, sliced
1 garlic clove, crushed
14oz can plum tomatoes
2 tbsp chopped fresh mint
1 tsp grated nutmeg
12oz young spinach leaves
10oz packet filo pastry
1 tsp sesame seeds
salt and black pepper

1 Preheat the oven to 400°F. Lightly brush a 8½ in round spring form pan with sunflower oil.

2 Cook the lamb and onion without fat in a non-stick pan until golden. Add the garlic, tomatoes, mint, nutmeg, and seasoning. Bring to a boil, stirring. Simmer, stirring occasionally, until most of the liquid has evaporated.

3 Wash the spinach and remove any tough stalks, then cook in only the water clinging to the leaves for about 2 minutes, until wilted.

4 Lightly brush each sheet of filo pastry with oil and lay in overlapping layers in the pan, leaving enough overhanging to wrap over the top.

5 Spoon in the meat and spinach, then wrap the pastry over to enclose, scrunching it slightly. Sprinkle with sesame seeds and bake for about 25–30 minutes, or until golden and crisp. Serve hot, with salad or vegetables.

COOK'S TIP

Choose filo pastry with large sheets, if possible. If yours aren't large enough to line the spring-form pan, arrange the smaller sheets two at a time in the tin, overlapping them slightly.

Pork Roast in a Blanket

INGREDIENTS

Serves 4

3lb lean pork loin joint
1 eating apple, cored and grated
¾ cup fresh bread crumbs
2 tbsp chopped hazelnuts
1 tbsp Dijon mustard
1 tbsp snipped fresh chives
salt and black pepper

1 If necessary, trim the roast, leaving only a thin layer of fat.

2 Preheat the oven to 425°F. Place the meat on a rack in a roasting pan, cover the meat with foil, and roast for 1 hour, then reduce the oven temperature to 350°F.

3 Mix together the apple, bread crumbs, nuts, mustard, chives, and seasoning. Remove the foil and spread the bread crumb mixture over the fat surface of the meat.

4 Roast the pork for 45–60 minutes, or until the juices run clear. Serve in slices with gravy.

VARIATION

For a change, use chopped almonds in place of the hazelnuts and substitute chopped fresh parsley for the chives.

Turkish Lamb and Apricot Stew

INGREDIENTS

Serves 4

1 large eggplant, cubed
2 tbsp sunflower oil
1 onion, chopped
1 garlic clove, crushed
1 tsp ground cinnamon
3 whole cloves
1lb boned leg of lamb, cubed
14oz can chopped tomatoes
²⁄₃ cup ready-to-eat dried apricots
4oz canned chick-peas, drained
1 tsp honey
salt and black pepper
3 cups cooked couscous, to serve
2 tbsp olive oil
2 tbsp chopped almonds, fried in a
 little oil
chopped fresh parsley

1 Place the eggplant in a colander, sprinkle with salt and leave for 30 minutes. Heat the oil in a flameproof casserole, add the onion and garlic and fry for 5 minutes, until softened.

2 Stir in the ground cinnamon and cloves and fry for 1 minute. Add the lamb and cook for 5–6 minutes, stirring occasionally, until well browned.

3 Rinse, drain and pat dry the eggplant, add to the pan and cook for 3 minutes, stirring well. Add the tomatoes, 1¼ cups water, the apricots and salt and pepper. Bring to a boil, then cover the pan and simmer gently for about 45 minutes.

4 Stir in the chick-peas and honey and cook for a further 15–20 minutes, or until the lamb is tender. Serve the stew accompanied by couscous with the olive oil, fried almonds and chopped parsley stirred in.

Country Pork with a Parsley Crust

This hearty casserole is a complete main course in one pot.

INGREDIENTS

Serves 4

1lb boneless pork shoulder, diced
1 small rutabaga, diced
2 carrots, sliced
2 parsnips, sliced
2 leeks, sliced
2 celery stalks, sliced
3⅔ cups boiling beef stock
2 tbsp tomato paste
2 tbsp chopped fresh parsley
¼ cup pearl barley
celery salt and black pepper

For the topping

1 cup flour
1 tsp baking powder
6 tbsp low fat ricotta
3 tbsp chopped fresh parsley

1 Preheat the oven to 350°F. Cook the pork without fat, in a non-stick pan until lightly browned.

2 Add the vegetables to the pan and stir over medium heat until lightly colored. Tip into a large casserole dish, then stir in the stock, tomato paste, parsley, and pearl barley.

3 Season with celery salt and pepper, then cover and place in the oven for about 1–1¼ hours, until the pork and vegetables are tender.

4 For the topping, sift the flour and baking powder with seasoning, then stir in the ricotta and parsley with enough cold water to mix to a soft dough. Roll out to about ½in thickness and cut into 12–16 triangles.

5 Remove the casserole from the oven and raise the oven temperature to 425°F.

6 Arrange the triangles over the casserole, overlapping. Bake for 15–20 minutes, until puffed and golden.

--- COOK'S TIP ---

When mixing the crust topping, add the water a little at a time, the dough should be soft, but not sticky. If it is slightly too damp, dust the work surface with a little flour before rolling out.

Pan-fried Mediterranean Lamb

The warm summery flavors of the Mediterranean are combined for a simple weekday meal.

INGREDIENTS 🍎

Serves 4
8 lean lamb rib chops
1 medium onion, thinly sliced
2 red bell peppers, seeded and sliced
14oz can plum tomatoes
1 garlic clove, crushed
3 tbsp chopped fresh basil leaves
2 tbsp chopped ripe olives
salt and black pepper

1 Trim any excess fat from the lamb, then cook without fat in a nonstick pan until golden brown.

2 Add the onion and bell peppers to the pan. Cook, stirring, for a few minutes to soften, then add the plum tomatoes, garlic, and basil.

3 Cover and simmer for 20 minutes or until the lamb is tender. Stir in the olives, season, and serve hot with pasta.

VARIATION

This recipe would be equally good with skinless chicken breast fillets instead of the lamb rib chops.

Bacon Koftas

These easy koftas are good for outdoor summer barbecues, served with lots of salad.

INGREDIENTS 🍎

Serves 4
8oz lean bacon, coarsely chopped
1 cup fresh whole-wheat
  bread crumbs
2 scallions, chopped
1 tbsp chopped fresh parsley
finely grated rind of 1 lemon
1 egg white
black pepper
paprika
lemon rind and fresh parsley leaves,
  to garnish

1 Place the bacon in a food processor together with the bread crumbs, scallions, parsley, lemon rind, egg white, and pepper. Process the mixture until it is finely chopped and begins to bind together.

2 Divide the bacon mixture into eight, even-sized pieces and shape into long ovals around eight wooden or bamboo skewers.

3 Sprinkle the koftas with paprika and cook under a hot broiler or on a barbecue for about 8–10 minutes, turning occasionally, until browned and cooked through. Garnish with lemon rind and parsley leaves, then serve hot with lemon rice and salad.

COOK'S TIP

Don't over-process the kofta mixture – it should be only just mixed. If you don't have a food processor, either grind the bacon, or chop it very finely by hand, then mix in the rest of the ingredients.

Louisiana Rice

INGREDIENTS

Serves 4

4 tbsp vegetable oil
1 small eggplant, diced
8oz ground pork
1 green bell pepper, seeded and chopped
2 stalks celery, chopped
1 onion, chopped
1 garlic clove, crushed
1 tsp cayenne pepper
1 tsp paprika
1 tsp black pepper
½ tsp salt
1 tsp dried thyme
½ tsp dried oregano
2 cups chicken stock
8oz chicken livers, finely chopped
¾ cup long grain rice
1 bay leaf
3 tbsp chopped fresh parsley
celery leaves, to garnish

1 Heat the oil in a frying pan until really hot, then add the eggplant and stir-fry for about 5 minutes.

2 Add the pork and cook for about 6–8 minutes, until browned, using a wooden spoon to break any lumps.

3 Add the pepper, celery, onion, garlic and all the spices and herbs. Cover and cook on a high heat for 5–6 minutes, stirring frequently from the bottom to scrape up and distribute the crispy brown bits.

4 Pour on the chicken stock and stir to clean the bottom of the pan. Cover and cook for 6 minutes over a moderate heat. Stir in the chicken livers, cook for 2 minutes, then mix in the rice and add the bay leaf.

5 Reduce the heat, cover and simmer for about 6–7 minutes. Turn off the heat and leave to stand for a further 10–15 minutes until the rice is tender. Remove the bay leaf and stir in the chopped parsley. Serve the rice hot, garnished with the celery leaves.

Moroccan Chicken Couscous

INGREDIENTS

Serves 4

1 tbsp butter
1 tbsp sunflower oil
4 chicken pieces
2 onions, finely chopped
2 garlic cloves, crushed
½ tsp ground cinnamon
¼ tsp ground ginger
¼ tsp ground turmeric
2 tbsp orange juice
2 tsp honey
salt and black pepper
fresh mint sprigs, to garnish

For the couscous

2¼ cups couscous
1 tsp salt
2 tsp sugar
2 tbsp sunflower oil
½ tsp ground cinnamon
pinch of grated nutmeg
1 tbsp orange blossom water
2 tbsp sultanas
½ cup chopped blanched almonds
3 tbsp chopped pistachio nuts

1 Heat the butter and oil in a large pan and add the chicken pieces, skin side down. Fry for 3–4 minutes, until the skin is golden, then turn over.

2 Add the onions, garlic, spices and a pinch of salt and pour over the orange juice and 1¼ cups water. Cover the pan and bring to a boil, then reduce the heat and simmer for about 30 minutes.

3 Meanwhile, place the couscous and salt in a bowl and cover with 1½ cups water. Stir once and leave the couscous to stand for 5 minutes. Add the sugar, 1 tbsp of the oil, the cinnamon, nutmeg, orange blossom water and sultanas to the couscous and mix very well.

4 Heat the remaining 1 tbsp of the oil in a pan and lightly fry the almonds until golden. Stir into the couscous with the pistachio nuts.

5 Line a steamer with parchment paper and spoon in the couscous. Sit the steamer over the chicken (or over a pan of boiling water) and steam for 10 minutes.

6 Remove the steamer and keep covered. Stir the honey into the chicken liquid and boil rapidly for 3–4 minutes. Spoon the couscous on to a warmed serving platter and top with the chicken, with a little of the sauce spooned over. Garnish with mint sprigs and serve with the remaining sauce.

Spiced Lamb with Apricots

INGREDIENTS

Serves 4

½ cup ready-to-eat dried apricots
⅓ cup seedless raisins
½ tsp saffron strands
⅔ cup orange juice
1 tbsp red wine vinegar
2–3 tbsp olive oil
3lb leg of lamb, boned and
   cubed
1 onion, chopped
2 garlic cloves, crushed
2 tsp ground cumin
¼ tsp ground cloves
1 tbsp ground coriander
2 tbsp flour
2½ cups lamb stock
3 tbsp chopped fresh coriander
salt and black pepper
saffron rice mixed with toasted
   almonds and chopped fresh
   coriander, to serve

1 Mix together the dried apricots, raisins, saffron, orange juice and vinegar in a bowl. Cover and leave to soak for 2–3 hours.

2 Preheat the oven to 325°F. Heat 2 tbsp oil in a large flameproof casserole and brown the lamb in batches. Remove and set aside. Add the onion and garlic with a little more of the remaining oil, if necessary, and cook until softened.

3 Stir in the spices and flour and cook for a further 1–2 minutes. Return the meat to the casserole. Stir in the stock, fresh coriander and the soaked fruit with its liquid. Add seasoning, then bring to a boil.

4 Cover the casserole and cook for 1½ hours (adding a little extra stock if necessary), or until the lamb is tender. Serve with saffron rice mixed with toasted almonds and fresh coriander.

Sausage and Bean Ragoût

An economical and nutritious main course that children will love. Garlic and herb bread makes an ideal accompaniment.

INGREDIENTS

Serves 4

2 cups dried cannellini or flageolet
   beans, soaked overnight
3 tbsp olive oil
1 onion, finely chopped
2 garlic cloves, crushed
1lb good-quality chunky sausages,
   skinned and thickly sliced
1 tbsp tomato paste
2 tbsp fresh chopped parsley
1 tbsp fresh chopped thyme
14oz can chopped tomatoes
salt and black pepper
chopped fresh thyme and parsley,
   to garnish

1 Drain and rinse the soaked beans and place them in a pan with enough water to cover. Bring to a boil, cover the pan and simmer for about 1 hour, or until tender. Drain the beans and set aside.

2 Heat the oil and fry the onion, garlic and sausages until golden.

3 Stir in the tomato paste, chopped parsley and thyme, tomatoes and seasoning, then bring to a boil.

4 Add the beans, then cover and cook gently for about 15 minutes, stirring occasionally, until the sausages are cooked through. Garnish with extra chopped fresh herbs and serve.

Lamb Pie with a Potato Crust

A pleasant change from meat and potatoes – healthier, too.

INGREDIENTS 🍎

Serves 4

1½lb potatoes, diced
2 tbsp skim milk
1 tbsp whole-grain or French mustard
1lb lean ground lamb
1 onion, chopped
2 celery stalks, sliced
2 carrots, diced
²/₃ cup beef stock
4 tbsp oatmeal
1 tbsp Worcestershire sauce
2 tbsp fresh chopped rosemary, or
  2 tsp dried
salt and black pepper

1 Cook the potatoes in boiling, lightly salted water until tender. Drain and mash until smooth, then stir in the milk and mustard. Meanwhile, preheat the oven to 400°F.

2 Break up the lamb with a fork and cook without fat in a nonstick pan until lightly browned. Add the onion, celery, and carrots to the pan and cook for 2–3 minutes, stirring.

3 Stir in the stock and oatmeal. Bring to a boil, then add the Worcestershire sauce and rosemary, and season to taste with salt and pepper.

4 Turn the meat mixture into a 7 cup ovenproof dish and spread over the potato topping evenly, swirling with the edge of a knife. Bake for 30–35 minutes, or until golden. Serve hot with fresh vegetables.

---— COOK'S TIP ———

You can prepare this pie up to a day ahead. Cover and chill until ready to bake. Allow the pie to come back to room temperature before baking, or add a few minutes extra cooking time.

Baked Pasta Bolognese

INGREDIENTS

Serves 4

2 tbsp olive oil
1 onion, chopped
1 garlic clove, crushed
1 carrot, diced
2 celery stalks, chopped
2 strips bacon, finely chopped
5 button mushrooms, chopped
1lb lean ground beef
½ cup red wine
1 tbsp tomato paste
7oz can chopped tomatoes
sprig of fresh thyme
2 cups dried penne pasta
1¼ cups milk
2 tbsp butter
2 tbsp flour
1 cup cubed mozzarella cheese
4 tbsp finely grated Parmesan cheese
salt and black pepper
a few small fresh basil sprigs,
   to garnish

1 Heat the oil in a pan and fry the onion, garlic, carrot and celery for 6 minutes, until the onion has softened.

2 Add the bacon and continue frying for 3–4 minutes. Stir in the mush-rooms, fry for 2 minutes, then add the beef. Fry on a high heat until well browned all over.

3 Pour in the red wine, the tomato paste dissolved in 3 tbsp water, and the tomatoes, then add the thyme and season well. Bring to a boil, cover the pan and simmer gently for about 30 minutes.

4 Preheat the oven to 400°F. Bring a large pan of water to a boil, add a little of the oil and cook the pasta for about 10 minutes.

5 Meanwhile, place the milk, butter and flour in a saucepan, heat gently and whisk continuously with a balloon whisk until thickened. Stir in the mozz-arella cheese and 2 tbsp of the grated Parmesan, and season lightly.

6 Drain the pasta when it is ready and stir into the cheese sauce. Uncover the Bolognese sauce and boil rapidly for 2 minutes to reduce the liquid.

7 Spoon the sauce into an ovenproof dish, top with the pasta mixture and sprinkle the remaining 2 tbsp Parmesan cheese evenly over the top. Bake for 25 minutes until golden. Garnish with basil and serve hot.

Curried Lamb and Lentils

This colorful curry is packed with protein and low in fat.

INGREDIENTS ●

Serves 4
8 lean, boneless lamb leg steaks, about 1¼lb total weight
1 medium onion, chopped
2 medium carrots, diced
1 celery stalk, chopped
1 tbsp hot curry paste
2 tbsp tomato paste
2 cups stock
1 cup green lentils
salt and black pepper
fresh coriander leaves, to garnish
boiled rice, to serve

1 In a large, non-stick pan, cook the lamb steaks without fat until browned, turning once.

2 Add the vegetables and cook for 2 minutes, then stir in the curry paste, tomato paste, stock, and lentils.

3 Bring to a boil, cover, and simmer gently for 30 minutes until tender. Add more stock, if necessary. Season and serve with coriander and rice.

— COOK'S TIP —

Use fresh lamb stock if you can for this curry, however a chicken or vegetable stock cube, dissolved in boiling water will work just as well.

Golden Pork and Apricot Casserole

The rich golden color and warm spicy flavor of this simple casserole make it ideal for chilly winter days.

INGREDIENTS ●

Serves 4
4 lean pork loin chops
1 medium onion, thinly sliced
2 yellow bell peppers, seeded and sliced
2 tsp medium hot curry powder
1 tbsp flour
1 cup chicken stock
⅔ cup dried apricots
2 tbsp whole-grain mustard
salt and black pepper

1 Trim the excess fat from the pork and cook without fat in a large, heavy or nonstick pan until lightly browned.

2 Add the onion and bell peppers to the pan and stir over moderate heat for 5 minutes. Stir in the curry powder and the flour.

3 Add the broth, stirring, then add the apricots and mustard. Cover and simmer for 25–30 minutes, until tender. Adjust the seasoning and serve hot, with rice or new potatoes.

— VARIATION —

To make Golden Lamb and Apricot Casserole, substitute lamb leg chops or steaks for the pork chops.

ROASTS, PIES & HOT-POTS

Slow-cooked, traditional recipes are everyone's favorite, and here you'll find time-honored classics such as Braised Brisket with Dumplings, and Steak, Kidney and Mushroom Pie, alongside less well known, but just as tasty, dishes like Butterflied Cumin and Garlic Lamb, and Pork Chops with Plums. There are also delicious twists on old-fashioned roasts, stews and casseroles to try, such as Beef Paprika with Roasted Peppers, or Herby Lamb Hot-pot – both are ideal for informal entertaining at the weekend.

Beef Paprika with Roasted Peppers

This dish is perfect for family suppers – roasting the peppers gives a new dimension.

Ingredients

Serves 4

2 tbsp olive oil
1½lb boneless stewing beef, cut into 1½in cubes
2 onions, chopped
1 garlic clove, crushed
1 tbsp flour
1 tbsp paprika, plus extra to garnish
14oz can chopped tomatoes
2 red bell peppers, halved and seeded
⅔ cup crème fraîche or sour cream
salt and black pepper
buttered noodles, to serve

1 Preheat the oven to 275°F. Heat the oil in a large flameproof casserole and brown the meat in batches. Remove the meat from the casserole using a slotted spoon.

2 Add the onions and garlic and fry gently until softened. Stir in the flour and paprika and continue cooking for a further 1–2 minutes, stirring.

3 Return the meat and any juices that have collected on the plate to the casserole, then add the chopped tomatoes and seasoning. Bring to a boil, stirring, then cover and cook in the oven for 2½ hours.

4 Meanwhile, place the peppers skin-side up on a broiling rack and broil until the skins have blistered and charred. Cool, then peel off the skins. Cut the flesh into strips. Add to the casserole and cook for a further 15–30 minutes, or until the meat is tender.

5 Stir in the crème fraîche or sour cream and sprinkle with paprika. Serve hot with buttered noodles.

— Cook's Tip —

Take care when browning the meat and add only a few pieces at a time. If you overcrowd the pan, steam is created and the meat will never brown!

Stuffed Beef Rolls

INGREDIENTS

Serves 4

2 tbsp butter
2 slices bacon, finely chopped
4oz mushrooms, chopped
1 tbsp chopped fresh parsley
grated rind and juice of 1 lemon
2 cups fresh bread crumbs
1½lb top round of beef, cut into
    8 thin slices
3 tbsp flour
3 tbsp oil
2 onions, sliced
scant 2 cups beef stock
salt and black pepper
chopped fresh parsley, to garnish

1 Preheat the oven to 325°F.
Heat the butter, add the bacon
and mushrooms and fry for about 3
minutes, then mix them with the
parsley, lemon rind and juice, bread
crumbs and seasoning.

2 Spread an equal amount of the
bread crumb mixture evenly over
the beef slices, leaving a narrow border
clear around the edge.

3 Roll up the slices and tie securely
with fine string, then dip the beef
rolls in the flour to coat lightly.

4 Heat the oil in a heavy shallow
pan, then fry the beef rolls until
lightly browned. Remove the beef
rolls from the pan and keep warm.

5 Add the onions to the pan and
fry until browned. Stir in the
remaining flour and cook until lightly
browned. Pour in the stock, stirring
constantly, then bring to the boil,
stirring and simmer for 2–3 minutes.

6 Transfer the beef rolls to a
casserole, pour over the sauce,
then cover the casserole tightly and
cook in the oven for 2 hours. Lift out
the rolls using a slotted spoon and
remove the string. Then return them
to the sauce and serve hot, garnished
with chopped parsley.

—— COOK'S TIP ——

At the end of the cooking the onions can
be puréed with a little of the stock, then
stirred back into the casserole to make a
smooth sauce, if you prefer.

Lamb, Leek and Apple Pie

INGREDIENTS

Serves 4

1½lb lamb neck fillets, cut into 12
 pieces
4oz bacon, diced
1 onion, thinly sliced
12oz leeks, sliced
1 large cooking apple, peeled, cored
 and sliced
¼–½tsp ground allspice
¼–½tsp freshly grated nutmeg
⅔ cup lamb, beef or vegetable stock
8oz ready-made pie pastry
beaten egg or milk, to glaze
salt and black pepper

1 Preheat the oven to 400°F. Layer
the meats, onion, leeks and apple
in a 3¾ cup pie dish, sprinkling in the
spices and seasoning as you go. Pour in
the stock.

2 Roll out the pastry to ¾in larger
than the top of the pie dish. Cut a
narrow strip from around the pastry, fit
it around the dampened rim of the
dish, then brush with water.

3 Lay the pastry over the dish, and
press the edges together to seal
them. Brush the top with beaten egg
or milk, and make a hole in the center.

4 Bake the pie for 20 minutes, then
reduce the oven temperature to
350°F and continue to bake for 1–1¼
hours, covering the pie with foil if the
pastry begins to become too brown.

Beef Wellington

Beef Wellington is supposedly so-
named because of the resemblance of
its shape and rich brown color to
the Duke of Wellington's boot.

INGREDIENTS

Serves 8

3lb fillet of beef
1 tbsp butter
2 tbsp oil
½ small onion, finely chopped
6oz mushrooms, chopped
6oz liver pâté
lemon juice
few drops of Worcestershire sauce
14oz ready-made puff pastry
salt and black pepper
beaten egg, to glaze

1 Preheat the oven to 425°F. Season
the beef with pepper, then tie it at
intervals with string.

2 Heat the butter and oil in a roasting
pan. Brown the beef over a high
heat, then cook in the oven for 20 minutes. Cool and remove the string.

3 Scrape the cooking juices into a
pan, add the onion and mushrooms and cook until tender. Cool,
then mix with the pâté. Add lemon
juice and Worcestershire sauce.

4 Roll out the pastry to a large ¼in
thick rectangle. Spread the pâté
mixture on the beef, then place it in
the centre of the pastry. Damp the
edges of the pastry, then fold over to
make a neat parcel, tucking in the
ends neatly; press to seal.

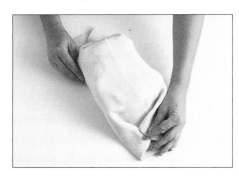

5 Place the parcel on a cookie sheet
with the join underneath and
brush with beaten egg. Bake for 25–45
minutes, depending how well done
you like the beef to be.

Oxtail Braised in Red Wine

Always plan to cook oxtail 1–2 days before you wish to eat it. This gives you time to skim off the fat before serving.

INGREDIENTS

Serves 3–4

4 tbsp sunflower oil
1 oxtail (about 2¼lb), cut in pieces
2 onions
2 carrots, quartered
2 celery stalks, cut in pieces
1¼ cups beef stock
1¼ cups red wine
bouquet garni
1 tbsp flour
8oz can chopped tomatoes
salt and black pepper
1 tbsp chopped fresh parsley, to garnish

1 Heat half the oil in a large flame-proof casserole or ovenproof pan with a tight-fitting lid. Sauté the pieces of oxtail until well browned.

2 Preheat the oven to 325°F. Add one of the onions, sliced, the pieces of carrot and celery, the stock, wine, bouquet garni, and seasoning. Bring to a boil and then transfer to the oven and cook for 1 hour.

3 Baste and stir well, reduce the oven temperature to 300°F for 1½–2 hours, or until the meat is very tender. Remove from the oven.

4 Leave to cool completely, then discard the surface fat and reheat. Remove the oxtail and reserve. Strain the stock and discard the vegetables. Preheat the oven to 350°F.

5 Fry the remaining onion, sliced, with the remaining oil in a large pan until golden. Stir in the flour and cook, stirring, until turning golden.

6 Gradually stir in the stock, a little at a time as it thickens. Bring back to the boil and then stir in the tomatoes. Add the oxtail, and seasoning to taste. Cover and cook in the oven for 30 minutes, or until the oxtail is heated through and really tender. Serve hot, sprinkled with the fresh parsley.

Braised Brisket with Dumplings

Brisket is very underrated and most often eaten as salt beef or pastrami these days. Given plenty of gentle cooking it produces a deliciously tender pot roast for eating hot with dumplings, or to serve cold with baked potatoes and salad.

INGREDIENTS

Serves 6–8
1 tbsp sunflower oil
2 onions, sliced
2lb piece of rolled brisket, tied
1¼ cups hot beef stock
1¼ cups beer
2 bay leaves
few parsley stalks
2 parsnips, chopped
2 carrots, sliced
½ rutabaga, chopped

For the dumplings
2 tbsp butter
1½ cups self-rising flour, sifted
1 tsp dry mustard
1 tsp each dried sage, thyme and
    parsley
salt and black pepper
fresh herb sprigs, such as parsley,
    oregano or thyme, to garnish

1 Preheat the oven to 325°F. Heat the oil in a large flameproof casserole or ovenproof pan and fry the onions until well browned.

2 Place the meat on top, then add the hot stock, the beer, bay leaves and parsley stalks and bring to the boil. Cover and transfer to the oven for 2 hours, basting occasionally.

3 Meanwhile, prepare the vegetables and make the dumplings. Rub the butter into the flour, then mix in the dry mustard, herbs and seasoning, and add sufficient water to mix to a soft dough mixture. Shape into about 12 small balls.

4 When the meat is just about tender, add the vegetables and cook for 20 minutes. Check the seasoning, add the dumplings and continue cooking for 15 minutes, until they are nicely swollen. Serve hot, garnished with herb sprigs.

Herby Lamb Hot-pot

Browning the lamb and kidneys, plus all the extra vegetables and herbs, adds flavor to the traditional basic ingredients.

INGREDIENTS

Serves 4

3 tbsp butter, or 3 tbsp oil
8 lamb chops, about 2lb total weight
6oz lamb's kidneys, cut into large
   pieces
2lb potatoes, thinly sliced
3 carrots, thickly sliced
1lb leeks, sliced
3 celery stalks, sliced
1 tbsp chopped fresh thyme
2 tbsp chopped fresh parsley
small sprig of rosemary
2½ cups veal stock
salt and black pepper

1 Preheat the oven to 325°F. Heat the butter or oil in a frying pan and brown the chops and kidneys in batches, then reserve the fat.

2 In a large casserole, make alternate layers of lamb chops, kidneys, three-quarters of the potatoes and the carrots, leeks and celery, sprinkling the herbs and seasoning over each layer as you go. Tuck the rosemary sprig down the side.

3 Arrange the remaining potatoes on top. Pour over the stock, brush with the reserved fat, then cover and bake for 2½ hours. Increase the oven temperature to 425°F. Uncover and cook for 30 minutes.

Pork Chops with Plums

INGREDIENTS

Serves 4

1lb ripe plums, halved and pitted
1¼ cups apple juice
3 tbsp butter
1 tbsp oil
4 pork chops, about 7oz each
1 onion, finely chopped
grated nutmeg
salt and black pepper
fresh sage leave, to garnish

1 Heat the butter and oil in a large frying pan and fry the chops until brown on both sides, then transfer them to a plate.

2 Meanwhile, simmer the plums in the apple juice until tender. Strain off and reserve the juice, then purée half the plums with a little of the juice.

3 Add the onion to the pan and cook gently until soft, but not coloured. Return the chops to the pan. Pour over the plum purée and all the juice.

4 Simmer, uncovered, for 10–15 minutes, until the chops are cooked through. Add the remaining plums to the pan, then add the nutmeg and seasoning. Warm the sauce through over a medium heat and serve garnished with fresh sage leaves.

COOK'S TIP

Use boneless pork steaks in place of the chops, if you like.

Roast Beef with Yorkshire Puddings

For this classic Sunday lunchtime meal, choose a joint of beef on the bone, such as sirloin or rib, or a boned and rolled joint of sirloin, rib or top round.

INGREDIENTS

Serves 6
4lb joint of beef
2–4 tbsp oil
¼ cups vegetable or veal stock, wine or water
salt and pepper

For the Yorkshire puddings
½ cup flour
1 egg, beaten
⅔ cup mixed water and milk
dripping or oil, for cooking

1 Weigh the beef and calculate the cooking time, allowing 15 minutes per 1lb plus 15 minutes for rare meat, 20 minutes plus 20 minutes for medium, and 25–30 minutes plus 25 minutes for well-done.

2 Preheat the oven to 425°F. Heat the oil in a roasting pan in the oven.

3 Place the meat on a rack, fat-side uppermost, then place the rack in the roasting pan.

4 Baste the beef with the oil, and cook for the required time, basting occasionally.

5 To make the Yorkshire puddings, stir the flour, salt and pepper together in a bowl and form a well in the center. Pour the egg into the well, then slowly pour in the milk, stirring in the flour to give a smooth batter. Leave to stand for 30 minutes.

6 A few minutes before the meat is ready, spoon a little oil in each of 12 muffin pans and place in the oven until very hot. Remove the meat from the oven, season, then cover loosely with foil and keep warm.

7 Quickly divide the batter among the muffin pans, then bake for 15–20 minutes, until well risen and brown.

8 Spoon off the fat from the roasting pan. Add the stock, wine or water, stirring to dislodge the sediment, and boil for a few minutes. Check the seasoning, then serve with the beef and Yorkshire puddings.

Irish Stew

INGREDIENTS

Serves 4

4 slices lean bacon, chopped
2 celery stalks, chopped
2 large onions, sliced
8 shoulder lamb chops, about
  2lb total weight
2lb potatoes, sliced
1¼ cups brown veal or beef stock
1½ tbsp Worcestershire sauce
1 tsp anchovy sauce
salt and black pepper
chopped fresh parsley, to garnish

1 Preheat the oven to 325°F. Fry the bacon for about 3–5 minutes until the fat runs, then add the celery and a third of the onions and cook, stirring occasionally, until softened and browned.

2 Layer the lamb chops, potatoes, vegetables and bacon and remaining onions in a heavy flameproof casserole, seasoning each layer, and finishing with a layer of potatoes.

3 Stir the veal or beef stock, Worcestershire sauce and anchovy sauce into the bacon and vegetable cooking juices in the pan and bring to a boil. Pour into the casserole, adding water if necessary so the liquid comes half way up the casserole.

4 Cover the casserole tightly, then cook in the oven for 3 hours, until the meat and vegetables are tender. Serve hot, sprinkled with chopped fresh parsley.

— COOK'S TIP —

The mutton that originally gave the flavour to Irish Stew is often difficult to obtain nowadays, so other flavorings are added to compensate.

Butterflied Cumin and Garlic Lamb

Ground cumin and garlic give the lamb a wonderful Middle-Eastern flavor, although you may prefer a simple oil, lemon and herb marinade instead.

INGREDIENTS

Serves 6
4lb leg of lamb
4 tbsp olive oil
2 tbsp ground cumin
4–6 garlic cloves, crushed
salt and black pepper
toasted almond and raisin-studded
   rice, to serve
coriander sprigs and lemon wedges,
   to garnish

1 To butterfly the lamb, cut away the meat from the bone using a small sharp knife. Remove any excess fat and the thin, parchment-like membrane. Bat out the meat to an even thickness, then prick the fleshy side of the lamb well with the tip of a knife.

2 In a bowl, mix together the oil, cumin and garlic and season with pepper. Spoon the mixture all over the lamb, then rub it well into the crevices. Cover and leave to marinate overnight.

3 Preheat the oven to 400°F. Spread the lamb, skin-side down, on a rack in a roasting pan. Season with salt and roast for 45–60 minutes, until crusty brown on the outside but still pink in the center.

4 Remove the lamb from the oven and leave it to rest for about 10 minutes. Cut into diagonal slices and serve with the toasted almond and raisin-studded rice. Garnish with coriander sprigs and lemon wedges.

COOK'S TIP

The lamb may be barbecued rather than broiled. Thread it on to two long skewers and set it on the barbecue grill. Barbecue for 20–25 minutes on each side, until it is cooked to your liking.

Pot-roast Pork with Celery

INGREDIENTS

Serves 4

1 tbsp oil
4 tbsp butter
about 2lb boned and rolled loin of
    pork, rind removed and well
    trimmed
1 onion, chopped
bouquet garni
3 sprigs fresh dill
²⁄₃ cup medium-bodied dry
    white wine
²⁄₃ cup water
stalks from 1 celery head, cut into
    1in lengths
2 tbsp flour
²⁄₃ cup heavy cream
squeeze of lemon juice
salt and black pepper
chopped fresh dill, to garnish

1 Heat the oil and half the butter in a heavy flameproof casserole just large enough to hold the pork and celery, then add the pork and brown evenly. Transfer the pork to a plate.

2 Add the onion to the casserole and cook until softened but not coloured. Place the bouquet garni and the dill sprigs on the onions, then place the pork on top and add any juices on the plate.

3 Pour the wine and water over the pork, season, cover tightly and simmer gently for 30 minutes.

4 Turn the pork, arrange the celery around it, then re-cover and continue to cook for about 40 minutes, until the pork and celery are tender.

5 Transfer the pork and celery to a warmed serving plate, cover and keep warm. Discard the bouquet garni and dill.

6 Mash the remaining butter with the flour, then whisk small pieces at a time into the cooking liquid while it is barely simmering. Cook for 2–3 minutes, stirring occasionally. Stir the cream into the casserole, bring to a boil and add a squeeze of lemon juice.

7 Slice the pork, pour some of the sauce over the slices and garnish with chopped dill. Serve the remaining sauce separately.

Beef in Guinness

INGREDIENTS

Serves 6

2lb boneless stewing beef, cut into
   1½in cubes
flour, for coating
3 tbsp oil
1 large onion, sliced
1 carrot, thinly sliced
2 celery stalks, thinly sliced
2 tsp sugar
1 tsp mustard powder
1 tbsp tomato paste
1 x 3in strip orange rind
bouquet garni
2½ cups Guinness
salt and black pepper

1 Toss the beef in flour to coat. Heat 2 tbsp oil in a large, shallow pan, then cook the beef in batches until lightly browned. Transfer to a bowl.

2 Add the remaining oil to the pan, then cook the onions until well browned, adding the carrot and celery towards the end.

3 Stir in the sugar, mustard, tomato paste, orange rind, Guinness and seasoning, then add the bouquet garni and bring to a boil. Return the meat, and any juices in the bowl, to the pan; add water, if necessary, so the meat is covered. Cover the pan tightly and cook gently for 2–2½ hours, until the meat is very tender.

Steak, Kidney and Mushroom Pie

INGREDIENTS

Serves 4

2 tbsp oil
1 onion, chopped
4oz bacon, chopped
1¼lb boneless stewing beef, cubed
2 tbsp flour
4oz lamb's kidneys
1⅔ cups beef stock
large bouquet garni
4oz button mushrooms
8oz ready-made puff pastry
beaten egg, to glaze
salt and black pepper

1 Preheat the oven to 325°F. Heat the oil in a heavy pan, then cook the bacon and onion until cooked and lightly browned.

2 Toss the beef in the flour. Stir the meat into the pan in batches and cook, stirring, until browned.

3 Toss the kidneys in flour and add to to the pan with the bouquet garni. Transfer to a casserole dish, then pour in the stock, cover and cook in the oven for 2 hours. Stir in the mushrooms and seasoning and leave to cool.

4 Preheat the oven to 425°F. Roll out the pastry on a lightly floured surface to about ¾in larger than the top of a 5 cup pie dish. Cut off a narrow strip from the pastry and fit around the dampened rim of the dish. Brush the pastry strip with water.

5 Tip the meat mixture, into the dish. Lay the pastry over the dish, press the edges together to seal, then knock them up with the back of a knife.

6 Make a small slit in the pastry, brush with beaten egg and bake for 20 minutes. Lower the oven temperature to 350°F and bake for a further 20 minutes, until the pastry is risen, golden and crisp.

Oatmeal and Herb Rack of Lamb

Ask the butcher to remove the chine bone for you (this is the long bone that runs along the eye of the meat) – this will make carving easier.

INGREDIENTS

Serves 6

2 racks of lamb, about 2lb each
finely grated rind of 1 lemon
4 tbsp medium oatmeal
1 cup fresh white bread crumbs
4 tbsp chopped fresh parsley
2 tbsp butter, melted
2 tbsp honey
salt and black pepper
roasted baby vegetables and gravy,
   to serve
fresh herb sprigs, to garnish

1 Preheat the oven to 400°F. Using a small sharp knife, carefully cut through the skin and meat about 1in from the tips of the bones. Pull off the fatty meat to expose the bones, then scrape around each bone tip until it is completely clean.

2 Trim all the skin and most of the fat off the meat, then lightly score the fat. Repeat with the second rack.

3 Mix together the lemon rind, oatmeal, bread crumbs, parsley and seasoning, then stir in the melted butter.

4 Brush the fatty side of each rack with honey, then press the oatmeal mixture evenly over the surface.

5 Place the racks in a roasting pan with the oatmeal sides uppermost. Roast for 40–50 minutes, depending on whether you like rare or medium lamb. Cover loosely with foil if browning too much. To serve, slice each rack into three and accompany with roasted baby vegetables and gravy made with the pan juices. Garnish with fresh herb sprigs.

Glazed Ham with Spiced Peaches

One of the most pleasing things about today's hams is there is so little waste. They're easy to cook, and can be served hot or cold, and make great leftovers.

INGREDIENTS

Serves 6
3–3½lb fresh or smoked ham
2½ cups cider
1 tbsp ground cinnamon
few black peppercorns, crushed
4–6 tbsp red currant jelly
15oz can peach slices in fruit juice
1 tsp five-spices powder
1 tbsp cider vinegar
sprigs of rosemary

1 If you prefer a smoked ham, be sure to soak it for at least 2 hours, or overnight first. Drain well.

2 Place the ham in a large pan with the cider, and add fresh water to cover. Add the cinnamon and peppercorns. Bring to a boil and simmer until cooked, allowing 20 minutes per 1lb and about 20 minutes over.

3 Preheat the oven to 400°F. Drain (saving the liquid), cool slightly, then cut away the skin neatly with a sharp knife. Score the fat, in diamonds, then coat with 2–4 tbsp of the red currant jelly. Transfer to a roasting pan and bake for 10 minutes until golden brown.

4 Meanwhile, make the spiced peaches; place ⅔ cup of the ham cooking liquid in a pan with the peach juice, spice, vinegar and 2 tbsp red currant jelly. Simmer for 10–15 minutes until syrupy. Add the peach slices and heat through. Serve the peacjes hot with the ham, garnished with sprigs rosemary.

COOK'S TIP

If you want a quicker serving accompaniment, choose a tasty fruit chutney, or buy ready-made spiced peaches or pears.

DINNER PARTY DISHES

The best recipes for entertaining are relatively easy to make, yet look and taste fantastic. Sizzling Chinese Steamed Fish certainly fits the bill and is well worth trying out. Other fish dishes such as Salmon with Watercress Sauce, and Sole with Cider and Cream would be equally good. While, if you would prefer a meaty main course, Mexican Spiced Roast Leg of Lamb, or Peppered Steaks with Madeira are certain to please.

Chinese Omelettes with Fried Rice

Ingredients

Makes 4

2 tbsp sesame oil
2 tbsp sesame seeds
1¼ cups cooked long grain rice
2in piece of cucumber, finely grated
1 tsp finely grated lemon rind
squeeze of lemon juice
6 eggs
1 tbsp dry sherry
1 tbsp light soy sauce
pinch of sugar
2 cups cooked, peeled shrimp
4 scallions, finely chopped
2 large tomatoes, seeded and chopped
2 tbsp vegetable oil
salt and black pepper
4 cooked shrimp in shells and fresh
    coriander sprigs, to garnish

1 Heat the sesame oil in a pan and fry the sesame seeds until golden. Stir in the cooked rice, followed by the cucumber, lemon rind and juice and seasoning. Cook for 2–3 minutes, then keep warm while making the omelettes.

2 Place the eggs, sherry, soy sauce, sugar and a little pepper into a bowl and beat with a fork. Stir in the peeled shrimp, scallions and tomatoes.

3 Heat ½ tbsp of the oil in frying pan and ladle in a quarter of the mixture. Fry over a moderate heat for 3–4 minutes, until the omelette is lightly golden underneath. Cover and cook until the omelette is just set.

4 Remove the lid and fold the omelette in half. Garnish with a shrimp and fresh coriander and serve with a spoonful of the rice. Make the remaining omelettes in the same way.

Sizzling Chinese Steamed Fish

Steamed whole fish is very popular in China and the wok is used as a steamer. In this recipe the fish is flavored with garlic, ginger and scallions cooked in sizzling hot oil.

Ingredients

Serves 4

4 rainbow trout (about 9oz each)
¼ tsp salt
½ tsp sugar
2 garlic cloves, finely chopped
1 tbsp finely diced fresh ginger root
5 scallions, cut into 2in lengths and
    finely shredded
4 tbsp groundnut oil
1 tsp sesame oil
3 tbsp light soy sauce
thread egg noodles, to serve

1 Make three diagonal slits on both sides of each fish and lay them on a heatproof plate. Place a small rack or trivet in a wok or large frying pan half filled with water, cover and heat until just simmering.

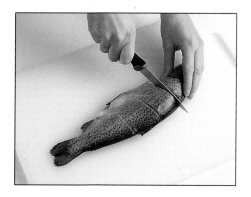

2 Sprinkle the fish with the salt, sugar, garlic and ginger. Sit the plate on the rack and cover. Steam gently for about 10–12 minutes, or until the flesh has turned pale pink and feels quite firm to the touch.

3 Turn off the heat, remove the lid and scatter the scallions over the fish. Replace the lid.

4 Heat the oils in a small pan over a high heat until just smoking, then quickly pour a quarter over the scallions on each of the fish – the shredded scallions will sizzle and cook in the hot oil – then sprinkle the soy sauce over the top. Serve the fish and juices immediately with boiled noodles.

Baked Cod with Tomatoes

For the best flavor, use firm ripe tomatoes for the sauce and make sure it is thick before spooning over the cod.

INGREDIENTS

Serves 4
2 tbsp olive oil
1 onion, chopped
2 garlic cloves, finely chopped
1lb tomatoes, peeled, seeded and
   chopped
1 tsp tomato paste
4 tbsp dry white wine
4 tbsp chopped flat leaf parsley
4 cod steaks
2 tbsp dried bread crumbs
salt and black pepper
new potatoes and green salad, to serve

1 Preheat the oven to 375°F. Heat the oil in a pan and fry the onion for about 5 minutes. Add the garlic, tomatoes, tomato paste, wine and seasoning. Bring just to a boil, then reduce the heat slightly and cook, uncovered, for about 15–20 minutes until thick. Stir in the chopped parsley.

2 Place the cod steaks in a shallow greased ovenproof dish and spoon an equal quantity of the tomato sauce on to each piece. Sprinkle the dried bread crumbs over the top.

3 Bake for 20–30 minutes, basting occasionally, until the bread crumbs are golden and crisp. Serve with new potatoes and a green salad.

Sole with Cider and Cream

INGREDIENTS

Serves 4
4 tbsp butter
1 onion, chopped
8 lemon sole fillets, about 4oz
   each, skinned
1¼ cups cider
⅔ cup fish stock
few parsley stalks
4oz button mushrooms, sliced
4oz cooked, peeled shrimp, defrosted
   if frozen
1 tbsp each flour and butter,
   blended together to make a
   beurre manié
½ cup heavy cream
salt and black pepper
chopped fresh parsley, to garnish

1 Melt 2 tbsp of the butter in a large frying pan with a lid. Add the chopped onion and fry gently, stirring occasionally, until softened.

2 Lightly season the fish, then fold each into three. Place the fish in the pan, and pour over the cider and stock. Tuck in the parsley stalks. Bring to simmering point, cover and cook for 7–10 minutes, until the fish is tender.

3 Meanwhile, melt the remaining butter and cook the mushrooms in a separate pan until tender. Transfer the fish to a warmed serving plate and scatter over the shrimp. Cover and keep warm while making the sauce.

4 Strain the fish cooking juices and return to the pan. Boil rapidly until slightly reduced. Add the beurre manié a little at a time, stirring until the sauce has thickened. Stir in the cream and seasoning to taste, then heat gently.

5 Spoon the cooked mushrooms over the fish, then pour over the cream sauce. Sprinkle with chopped fresh parsley and serve at once.

Mediterranean Fish Stew

INGREDIENTS

Serves 4

2 cups cooked shrimp in shells

1lb mixed white fish fillets such as cod, whiting, haddock, mullet or monk-fish skinned and chopped (reserve skins for the stock)

3 tbsp olive oil

1 onion, chopped

1 leek, sliced

1 carrot, diced

1 garlic clove, chopped

½ tsp ground turmeric

⅔ cup dry white wine or apple cider

14oz can chopped tomatoes

sprig each of fresh parsley, thyme and fennel

1 bay leaf

small piece of orange peel

1 cleaned squid, body cut into rings and tentacles chopped

12 mussels in shells

salt and black pepper

2–3 tbsp Parmesan cheese shavings, to sprinkle

chopped fresh parsley, to garnish

For the rouille sauce

2 slices white bread, crusts removed

2 garlic cloves, crushed

½ fresh red chili

1 tbsp tomato paste

3–4 tbsp olive oil

1 Peel the shrimp leaving the tails on; cover and chill. Place all the shrimp trimmings and fish trimmings in a pan and cover with 1⅞ cups water. Bring to a boil, then cover the pan and simmer for approximately 30 minutes. Strain and reserve the stock.

2 Heat the oil in a large saucepan and add the onion, leek, carrot and garlic. Fry gently for 6–7 minutes, then stir in the turmeric. Pour on the white wine, tomatoes and juice, the reserved fish stock, the herbs and orange peel. Bring to a boil, then cover and simmer gently for about 20 minutes.

3 Meanwhile, prepare the rouille sauce. Blend the bread in a food processor with the garlic, chili and tomato paste. With the motor running, pour in the oil in a thin drizzle until the mixture is smooth and thickened.

4 Add the fish and seafood to the pan and simmer for 5–6 minutes, or until the fish is opaque and the mussels are open. Remove the bay leaf and peel. Season the stew and serve in bowls with a spoonful of the rouille sauce, and sprinkled with Parmesan and parsley.

Salmon with Watercress Sauce

Adding the watercress right at the end of cooking retains much of its flavor and color.

INGREDIENTS

Serves 4

1¼ cups heavy cream
2 tbsp chopped fresh tarragon
2 tbsp unsalted butter
1 tbsp sunflower oil
4 salmon fillets, skinned and boned
1 garlic clove, crushed
½ cup dry white wine
1 bunch watercress
salt and black pepper

1 Gently heat the cream in a small pan until just beginning to boil. Remove the pan from the heat and stir in half the tarragon. Leave the herb cream to infuse while you cook the fish.

2 Heat the butter and oil in a frying pan, add the salmon and fry for 3–5 minutes on each side. Remove from the pan and keep warm.

3 Add the garlic and fry for 1 minute, then pour in the wine and let it bubble until reduced to about 1 tbsp.

4 Meanwhile, strip the leaves off the watercress stalks and chop finely. Discard any damaged leaves. (Save the watercress stalks for soup, if you like.)

5 Strain the herb cream into the pan and cook for a few minutes, stirring until the sauce has thickened. Stir in the remaining tarragon and watercress, then cook for a few minutes, until wilted but still bright green. Season and serve at once, spooned over the salmon.

Middle Eastern Lamb Kabobs

Skewered, grilled meats are the main item in many Middle Eastern and Greek restaurants. In this recipe marinated lamb is grilled with vegetables.

INGREDIENTS

Makes 4

1lb boneless leg of lamb, cubed
5 tbsp olive oil
1 tbsp chopped fresh oregano or
   thyme, or 2 tsp dried oregano
1 tbsp chopped fresh parsley
juice of ½ lemon
½ small eggplant, quartered and
thickly sliced
4 baby onions, halved
2 tomatoes, quartered
4 fresh bay leaves
salt and black pepper
pita bread and natural yogurt,
   to serve

1 Place the lamb in a bowl. Mix together the olive oil, oregano, parsley, lemon juice and seasoning, pour over the lamb and mix well. Cover and marinate for about 1 hour.

2 Preheat the broiler. Thread the marinated lamb, eggplant, onions, tomatoes and bay leaves alternately on to four large skewers.

3 Place the kabobs on a broiling rack and brush the vegetables liberally with the leftover marinade. Cook the kebabs under a medium heat for about 8–10 minutes on each side, basting once or twice with the juices that have collected in the bottom of the broiling pan. Serve the kabobs hot, with hot pita bread and natural yogurt.

COOK'S TIP

Make a lemony bulgur wheat salad to accompany the kabobs if you like. Or serve them with plain, boiled rice – either basmati or jasmine rice would be a good choice.

Mexican Spiced Roast Leg of Lamb

INGREDIENTS

Serves 4

1 small leg or half leg (about
   2½lb) lamb
1 tbsp dried oregano
1 tsp ground cumin
1 tsp hot chili powder
2 garlic cloves
3 tbsp olive oil
2 tbsp red wine vinegar
salt and black pepper
fresh oregano sprigs, to garnish

1 Preheat the oven to 425°F. Place the leg of lamb on a large cutting board.

2 Place the oregano, cumin, chili powder and one of the garlic cloves, crushed, into a bowl. Pour on half of the olive oil and mix well to form a paste. Set the paste aside.

3 Using a sharp knife, make a criss-cross pattern of fairly deep slits through the skin and just into the meat.

4 Press the spice paste into the meat slits with the back of a knife.

5 Slice the remaining garlic clove thinly and cut each slice in half again. Push the pieces of garlic deeply into the slits in the meat (to prevent burning during roasting).

6 Mix the vinegar and remaining oil, pour over the joint and season with salt and freshly ground black pepper.

7 Bake the lamb for about 15 minutes at the higher temperature, then reduce the heat to 350°F and cook for a further 1¼ hours (or a little longer if you like your meat well done). Serve the lamb with a delicious gravy made with the spicy pan juices and garnish with fresh oregano sprigs.

Peking Beef and Pepper Stir-fry

INGREDIENTS

Serves 4

12oz rump or sirloin steak, sliced
   into strips
2 tbsp soy sauce
2 tbsp medium sherry
1 tbsp cornstarch
1 tsp brown sugar
1 tbsp sunflower oil
1 tbsp sesame oil
1 garlic clove, finely chopped
1 tbsp grated fresh ginger root
1 red bell pepper, seeded and sliced
1 yellow bell pepper, seeded and sliced
4oz sugar snap peas
4 scallions, diagonally cut into
   2in pieces
2 tbsp Chinese oyster sauce
hot noodles, to serve

1 In a bowl, mix together the steak strips, soy sauce, sherry, cornstarch and brown sugar. Cover and leave to marinate for 30 minutes.

2 Heat the oils in a wok or large frying pan. Add the garlic and ginger and stir-fry quickly for about 30 seconds. Add the peppers, sugar snap peas and scallions and stir-fry over a high heat for 3 minutes.

3 Add the beef with the marinade juices to the wok or frying pan and stir-fry for a further 3–4 minutes.

4 Finally, pour in the oyster sauce and 4 tbsp water and stir until the sauce has thickened slightly. Serve immediately with hot noodles.

Texan Barbecued Ribs

An American favorite of pork spare ribs cooked in a sweet and sour barbecue sauce. Ideal as a barbecue dish, this can be just as easily cooked in the oven and makes an excellent choice for a casual dinner party.

INGREDIENTS

Serves 4

3lb (about 16) lean pork spare ribs
1 onion, finely chopped
1 large garlic clove, crushed
½ cup tomato catsup
2 tbsp orange juice
2 tbsp red wine vinegar
1 tsp mustard
2 tsp honey
2 tbsp soft light brown sugar
dash of Worcestershire sauce
2 tbsp vegetable oil
salt and black pepper
chopped fresh parsley, to garnish

1 Preheat the oven to 400°F. Place the lean pork spare ribs in a large shallow roasting pan and then bake, uncovered, for 20 minutes.

2 Meanwhile, mix together the onion, garlic, tomato catsup, orange juice, red wine vinegar, mustard, honey, brown sugar, Worcestershire sauce, oil and seasoning in a pan. Bring to a boil, then reduce the heat and simmer gently for about 5 minutes.

3 Remove the ribs from the oven and reduce the temperature to 350°F. Spoon over half the sauce, covering the ribs well, and bake for 20 minutes. Turn the ribs over, baste with the remaining sauce and cook in the oven for a further 25 minutes.

4 Sprinkle the ribs with parsley and serve three or four ribs per person. Provide small finger bowls for washing sticky fingers.

Breton Pork and Bean Casserole

INGREDIENTS

Serves 4

2 tbsp olive oil
1 onion, chopped
2 garlic cloves, chopped
1lb lean shoulder of pork, cubed
12oz lean lamb (preferably leg),
    trimmed and cubed
8oz coarse pork and garlic sausage,
    cut into chunks
14oz can chopped tomatoes
2 tbsp red wine
1 tbsp tomato paste
bouquet garni
14oz can cannellini beans, drained
1 cup whole wheat bread
    crumbs
salt and black pepper
salad and French bread, to serve

1 Preheat the oven to 325°F. Heat the oil in a large flameproof casserole and fry the chopped onion and garlic until softened. Remove with a slotted spoon and reserve.

2 Add the pork, lamb and sausage to the pan and fry on a high heat until browned on all sides. Return the onion and garlic to the pan.

3 Stir in the chopped tomatoes, wine and tomato paste and add 1¼ cups water. Season well and put in the bouquet garni.

4 Cover and bring to a boil, then transfer the casserole to the pre-heated oven and cook for 1½ hours.

5 Remove the bouquet garni, stir in the beans and sprinkle the bread crumbs over the top. Return to the oven, uncovered, for a further 30 minutes, until the top is golden brown. Serve hot with a green salad and French bread to mop up the juices.

COOK'S TIP

Replace the lamb with duck breast, if you like, but be sure to drain off any fat before sprinkling with the bread crumbs.

Peppered Steaks with Madeira

A really easy special-occasion dish. Mixed peppercorns have an excellent flavor, though black pepper will, of course, do instead.

INGREDIENTS

Serves 4

1 tbsp mixed dried peppercorns
   (green, pink and black)
4 fillet or sirloin steaks, about
   6oz each
1 tbsp olive oil, plus extra
   for frying
1 garlic clove, crushed
4 tbsp Madeira
6 tbsp fresh beef stock
⅔ cup heavy cream
salt

1 Finely crush the peppercorns using a pestle and mortar, then press on to both sides of the steaks.

2 Place the steaks in a shallow non-metallic dish, then add the oil, garlic and Madeira. Cover and leave to marinate in a cool place for 4–6 hours, or preferably overnight.

3 Remove the steaks from the dish, reserving the marinade. Brush a little oil over a heavy-based frying pan and heat until hot.

4 Add the steaks and cook over a high heat, allowing 3 minutes per side for medium or 2 minutes per side for rare. Remove and keep warm.

5 Add the reserved marinade and the stock to the pan and bring to the boil, then leave the sauce to bubble until it is well reduced.

6 Add the cream, with salt to taste, to the pan and stir until slightly thickened. Serve the steaks on warmed plates with the sauce.

Ginger Pork with Black Bean Sauce

INGREDIENTS

Serves 4

12oz pork fillet
1 garlic clove, crushed
1 tbsp grated fresh ginger root
6 tbsp chicken stock
2 tbsp dry sherry
1 tbsp light soy sauce
1 tsp sugar
2 tsp cornstarch
3 tbsp groundnut oil
2 yellow bell peppers, seeded and cut
   into strips
2 red bell peppers, seeded and cut
   into strips
1 bunch scallions, diagonally sliced
3 tbsp preserved black beans, coarsely
   chopped
coriander sprigs, to garnish

1 Cut the pork into thin slices across the grain of the meat. Put the slices into a dish and mix them with the garlic and ginger. Leave to marinate at room temperature for 15 minutes.

2 Blend together the stock, sherry, soy sauce, sugar and cornstarch in a small bowl, then set the sauce mixture aside.

3 Heat the oil in a wok or large frying pan, add the marinated pork and stir-fry for 2–3 minutes. Add the peppers and scallions and stir-fry for a further 2 minutes.

4 Add the beans and sauce mixture and cook, stirring until thick. Serve hot, garnished with coriander.

Asparagus and Ham Gratin

Choose plump green asparagus spears and the best cooked ham for this tasty gratin – it's a good way of stretching a small quantity of asparagus! Serve with warm crusty bread.

INGREDIENTS

Serves 4

12 asparagus spears
6 slices baked ham, halved
3 tbsp butter
⅓ cup flour
1⅞ cups milk
2 tsp Dijon mustard
3oz Gruyère cheese, grated
freshly grated nutmeg
1oz Parmesan cheese, finely grated
7 tbsp fresh fine white bread crumbs
salt and black pepper

1 Preheat the oven to 375°F. Trim the woody ends from the asparagus, then place the spears in a large frying pan with about 1in boiling water. Cover the pan and cook for 4 minutes, then drain thoroughly.

2 Wrap a slice of baked ham around each asparagus spear and arrange in a shallow buttered ovenproof dish.

3 Melt the butter in a pan. Add the flour and cook for 1 minute, stirring. Gradually add the milk, then bring to a boil, stirring to give a smooth sauce. Stir in the mustard, Gruyère, salt, pepper and nutmeg to taste.

4 Pour the sauce over the asparagus. Mix the Parmesan cheese with the bread crumbs and sprinkle evenly over the top. Bake for about 20 minutes, until browned on top and bubbling. Serve immediately.

Pork with Mozzarella and Sage

Here is a variation of a famous Italian dish *Saltimbocca alla Romana* – the mozzarella adds a delicious creamy flavor.

INGREDIENTS

Serves 2–3
8oz pork tenderloin
1 garlic clove, crushed
3oz mozzarella cheese, cut into
    6 slices
6 slices prosciutto
6 large sage leaves
2 tbsp unsalted butter
salt and black pepper
potato wedges roasted in olive oil, and
    green beans, to serve

1 Trim any excess fat from the pork, then cut the pork crosswise into six pieces about 1in thick.

2 Stand each piece of tenderloin on end and bat down with a rolling pin to flatten. Rub with garlic and set aside for 30 minutes in a cool place.

3 Place a slice of mozzarella on top of each pork steak and season with salt and pepper. Lay a slice of prosciutto on top of each, crinkling it a little to fit.

4 Press a sage leaf on to each and secure with a toothpick. Melt the butter in a large heavy-based frying pan. Add the pork and cook for about 2 minutes on each side until you see the mozzarella melting. Remove the toothpicks and serve immediately with the potatoes and green beans.

Red currant-glazed Lamb Chops

Loin chops could be used instead of the rib chops to make this dish more economical.

INGREDIENTS

Serves 4
8 lamb rib chops, about 1in thick
2 tbsp olive oil
2 tbsp red wine
½ garlic clove, chopped
4 tbsp red currant jelly
grated rind of 1 orange
2 tbsp chopped fresh mint
black pepper

1 Place the lamb chops in a shallow dish. To make the marinade, mix together the olive oil, red wine and garlic in a bowl, then season to taste with plenty of black pepper.

2 Pour the marinade over the meat, and leave to marinate for 1 hour.

3 Put the red currant jelly and orange rind in a small pan and stir over a low heat until the jelly melts. Remove from the heat and stir in the mint.

4 Lift the lamb chops from the marinade and arrange on a broiling rack. Broil or barbecue for 10–15 minutes, according to whether you like your lamb rare or medium cooked, turning occasionally and brushing frequently with the red currant glaze.

Five-spice Lamb

This aromatic lamb dish is perfect for an informal supper party.

INGREDIENTS

Serves 4

2–3 tbsp oil
3–3½lb leg of lamb, boned
  and cubed
1 onion, chopped
2 tsp grated fresh ginger root
1 garlic clove, crushed
1 tsp five-spice powder
2 tbsp hoisin sauce
1 tbsp light soy sauce
1¼ cups crushed tomatoes
1 cup lamb stock
1 red bell pepper, seeded and cubed
1 yellow bell pepper, seeded and cubed
2 tbsp chopped fresh coriander
1 tbsp sesame seeds, toasted
salt and black pepper

1 Preheat the oven to 325°F. Heat 2 tbsp of the oil in a flameproof casserole and then brown the lamb in batches over a high heat. Remove the meat and set aside.

2 Add the onion, ginger and garlic to the casserole with a little more of the oil, if necessary, and cook for about 5 minutes, until softened.

3 Return the lamb to the casserole. Stir in the five-spice powder, hoisin and soy sauces, crushed tomatoes, stock and seasoning. Bring to a boil, then cover and cook in the oven for 1¼ hours.

4 Remove the casserole from the oven, stir in the peppers, then cover and return to the oven for a further 15 minutes, or until the lamb is very tender.

5 Sprinkle with the coriander and sesame seeds. Serve hot.

Pork Steaks with Gremolata

Gremolata is a popular Italian dressing of garlic, lemon and parsley – it adds a hint of sharpness to the pork.

INGREDIENTS

Serves 4
2 tbsp olive oil
4 pork shoulder steaks
1 onion, chopped
2 garlic cloves, crushed
2 tbsp tomato paste
14oz can chopped tomatoes
²⁄₃ cup dry white wine
bouquet garni
3 anchovy fillets, drained and chopped
salt and black pepper
salad leaves, to serve

For the gremolata
3 tbsp chopped fresh parsley
grated rind of ½ lemon
grated rind of 1 lime
1 garlic clove, chopped

1 Heat the oil in a large flameproof casserole, add the pork steaks and brown on both sides. Remove the steaks from the casserole.

2 Add the onion to the casserole and cook until soft and beginning to brown. Add the garlic and cook for 1–2 minutes, then stir in the tomato paste, chopped tomatoes and wine. Add the bouquet garni. Bring to a boil, then boil rapidly for 3–4 minutes to reduce and thicken slightly.

3 Return the pork to the casserole, then cover and cook for about 30 minutes. Stir in the chopped anchovies.

4 Cover the casserole and cook for a further 15 minutes, or until the pork is tender. Meanwhile, to make the gremolata, mix together the parsley, lemon and lime rinds and garlic.

5 Remove the pork steaks and discard the bouquet garni. Reduce the sauce over a high heat, if it is not already thick. Taste and adjust the seasoning.

6 Return the pork to the casserole, then sprinkle with the gremolata. Cover and cook for a further 5 minutes, then serve hot with salad leaves.

Pasta with Chicken Livers

INGREDIENTS

Serves 4

8oz chicken livers, defrosted
    if frozen
2 tbsp olive oil
2 garlic cloves, crushed
6oz hickory smoked bacon, coarsely
    chopped
14oz can chopped tomatoes
⅔ cup chicken stock
1 tbsp tomato paste
1 tbsp dry sherry
2 tbsp chopped fresh mixed herbs, such
    as parsley, rosemary and basil
12oz dried orecchiette pasta
salt and black pepper
freshly grated Parmesan cheese,
    to serve

1 Wash and trim the chicken livers. Cut into bite-sized pieces. Heat the oil in a sauté pan and fry the chicken livers for 3–4 minutes.

2 Add the garlic and bacon to the pan and fry until golden brown. Add the tomatoes, chicken stock, tomato paste, sherry, herbs and seasoning.

3 Bring to a boil and simmer gently, uncovered, for about 5 minutes until the sauce has thickened.

4 Meanwhile, cook the orecchiette in boiling salted water for about 12 minutes until al dente. Drain well, then toss into the sauce. Serve hot, sprinkled with Parmesan cheese.

— COOK'S TIP —

You'll find *orecchiette*, a dried pasta shaped like ears or flying saucers, in most large supermarkets.

Chicken Baked in a Salt Crust

This unusual dish is extremely easy to make. Once cooked, you just break away the salt crust to reveal the wonderfully tender, golden brown chicken.

INGREDIENTS

Serves 4

3–3½lb free-range oven-ready
    chicken
bunch of mixed fresh herbs, such
    as rosemary, thyme, marjoram
    and parsley
about 3–3½lb/10 cups coarse sea
    salt or kosher salt
1 egg white
1–2 whole heads of baked garlic,
    to serve

1 Wipe the chicken and remove the giblets. Put the herbs into the cavity, then truss the chicken.

2 Mix together the sea salt and egg white until all the salt crystals are moistened. Select a roasting pan into which the chicken will fit neatly, then line it with a large double layer of foil.

3 Spread a thick layer of moistened salt in the foil-lined pan and place the chicken on top. Cover with the remaining salt and press into a neat shape, over and around the chicken, making sure it is completely enclosed.

4 Bring the foil edges up and over the chicken to enclose it and bake in the oven for 1½ hours. Remove from the oven and leave to rest for 10 minutes.

5 Carefully lift the foil package from the container and open. Break the salt crust to reveal the chicken inside. Brush any traces of salt from the bird, then serve with baked whole heads of garlic. Each clove can be slipped from its skin and eaten with a bite of chicken.

Ruby Pork Chops

This sweet, tangy sauce works well with lean pork chops.

INGREDIENTS 🍎

Serves 4

1 ruby grapefruit
4 lean boneless pork chops
3 tbsp red currant jelly
salt and black pepper

COOK'S TIP

Choose a really juicy grapefruit and make sure that you pare away all the white pith when you peel it otherwise the sauce will be bitter.

1 Cut away all the peel and pith from the grapefruit, using a sharp knife, and carefully remove the segments, catching the juice in a bowl.

2 Cook the pork chops in a nonstick skillet without fat, turning them once, until golden and cooked.

3 Add the reserved grapefruit juice and red currant jelly to the pan and stir until melted. Add the grapefruit segments, then season with salt and pepper, and serve hot with vegetables.

Jamaican Bean Stew

If pumpkin is not available, use any other type of squash, or try rutabaga instead. This recipe is a good one to double – or even triple – for a crowd.

INGREDIENTS 🍎

Serves 4

1lb stewing beef, diced
1 small pumpkin, about 1lb, flesh diced
1 medium onion, chopped
1 green bell pepper, seeded and sliced
1 tbsp paprika
2 garlic cloves, crushed
1in piece fresh ginger root, chopped
14oz can chopped tomatoes
1 cup baby corn
1 cup beef stock
15oz can chick-peas, drained
15oz can red kidney beans, drained
salt and black pepper

3 Stir in the tomatoes, corn, and stock, then bring to a boil. Cover and simmer for 40–45 minutes or until tender. Add the chick-peas and beans, and heat thoroughly. Adjust the seasoning with salt and pepper to taste. Serve hot, with couscous or rice.

1 Cook the diced beef without fat in a large flameproof casserole, stirring to seal it on all sides.

2 Stir in the pumpkin, onion, and pepper, cook for 2 minutes more, then add the paprika, garlic, and ginger.

VARIATION

If there aren't any baby corn available, then use a small can of corn kernels instead and add to the stew with the chick-peas and kidney beans.

INDEX

Apples: lamb, leek and apple pie, 58
Apricots: golden pork and apricot
     casserole, 52
   spiced lamb with apricots, 48
   Turkish lamb and apricot stew, 42
Artichokes: chick-peas and artichokes au
   gratin, 24
Asparagus and ham gratin, 86

Bacon: bacon and egg bread pudding, 24
   bacon koftas, 44
   baked pasta Bolognese, 51
   mushroom and bacon risotto, 38
   pasta carbonara, 16
Baked cod with tomatoes, 76
Baked macaroni and cheese, 16
Baked pasta Bolognese, 51
Basil: tagliatelle with hazelnut pesto, 28
Batter: pork and celery popovers, 18
   roast beef with Yorkshire puddings, 64
   toad in the hole, 22
Beef: baked pasta Bolognese, 51
   beef and mushroom burgers, 23
   beef in Guinness, 68
   stuffed beef rolls, 57
   beef paprika with roasted peppers, 56
   beef strips with orange and ginger, 27
   beef Wellington, 58
   braised brisket with dumplings, 61
   Cornish pasties, 19
   Jamaican bean stew, 94
   ground beef pie with garlic potatoes, 39
   Peking beef and pepper stir-fry, 82
   peppered steaks with Madeira, 85
   rich beef casserole, 32
   roast beef with Yorkshire puddings, 64
   steak, kidney and mushroom pie, 68
Bell peppers: beef paprika with roasted
     peppers, 56
   lamb's liver with peppers, 36
   Peking beef and pepper stir-fry, 82
Black beans: ginger pork with black
     bean sauce, 86
Braised brisket with dumplings, 61
Bread: bacon and egg bread pudding, 24
Breton pork and bean casserole, 84
Butterflied cumin and garlic lamb, 66

Cannellini beans: Breton pork and bean
   casserole, 84
Casseroles and stews: beef in Guinness, 68
   beef paprika with roasted peppers, 56
   Breton pork and bean casserole, 84
   country pork with a parsley crust, 43
   five-spice lamb, 90
   golden pork and apricot casserole, 52
   herby lamb hot-pot, 62
   Irish stew, 65
   Jamaican bean stew, 94
   Mediterranean fish stew, 78
   pot-roast pork with celery, 67
   rich beef casserole, 32
   Turkish lamb and apricot stew, 42
Cauliflower cheese, 20
Celery: pork and celery popovers, 18
pot-roast pork with celery, 67
Cheese: asparagus and ham gratin, 86

baked macaroni and cheese, 16
   cauliflower cheese, 20
   golden cheese pudding, 20
   pasta carbonara, 16
   pork with Mozzarella and sage, 88
   tagliatelle with hazelnut pesto, 28
Chick-peas: chick-peas and artichokes
   au gratin, 24
   Jamaican bean stew, 94
Chicken: chicken baked in a salt crust, 92
   Moroccan chicken couscous, 47
Chicken livers: pasta with chicken livers,
   92
Chinese omelettes with fried rice, 74
Cod: baked cod with tomatoes, 76
Corned beef and egg hash, 26
Cornish pasties, 19
Couscous: Moroccan chicken couscous,
   47
Curried lamb and lentils, 52

Dumplings: braised brisket with
     dumplings, 61
   sausages and beans with dumplings, 35

Eggs: bacon and egg bread pudding, 24
   Chinese omelettes with fried rice, 74
   corned beef and egg hash, 26
   kedgeree, 14
   pasta carbonara, 16
   Mediterranean fish stew, 78

Five-spice lamb, 90
Flageolet beans: sausage and bean
   ragoût, 48

Garlic: butterflied cumin and garlic
     lamb, 66
   ground beef pie with garlic potatoes, 39
Ginger: beef strips with orange and
     ginger, 27
   ginger pork with black bean sauce, 86
Golden cheese pudding, 20
Golden pork and apricot casserole, 52
Grapefruit: ruby pork chops, 94
Greek lamb pie, 40
Gremolata: pork steaks with gremolata,
   91
Ham: asparagus and ham gratin, 86
   glazed ham with spiced peaches, 71
   pasta carbonara, 16
Hazelnuts: tagliatelle with hazelnut
   pesto, 28
Herbs: herby lamb hot-pot, 62
   oatmeal and herb rack of lamb, 70

Irish stew, 65

Jamaican bean stew, 94

Kabobs: Middle Eastern lamb kabobs, 80
Kedgeree, 14
Kidney beans: Jamaican bean stew, 94
   sausages and beans with dumplings, 35

Kidneys: steak, kidney and mushroom
   pie, 68

Lamb: Breton pork and bean casserole,
     84
   butterflied cumin and garlic lamb, 66
   curried lamb and lentils, 52
   five-spice lamb, 90
   Greek lamb pie, 40
   herby lamb hot-pot, 62
   Irish stew, 65
   lamb pie with a potato crust, 50
   lamb steaks with mint dressing, 34
   lamb's liver with peppers, 36
   lamb, leek and apple pie, 58
   Mexican spiced roast leg of lamb, 80
   Middle Eastern lamb kabobs, 80
   oatmeal and herb rack of lamb, 70
   pan-fried Mediterranean lamb, 44
   red currant-glazed lamb chops, 88
   spiced lamb with apricots, 48
   Turkish lamb and apricot stew, 42
Leeks: lamb, leek and apple pie, 58
Lemon: noodles with prawns in lemon
   sauce, 15
Lentils: curried lamb and lentils, 52
Liver: lamb's liver with peppers, 36
   liver and onions, 33
   Louisiana rice, 46

Macaroni: baked macaroni and
   cheese,16
Mediterranean fish stew, 78
Mexican spiced roast leg of lamb, 80
Middle Eastern lamb kabobs, 80
Mint: Greek lamb pie, 40
   lamb steaks with mint dressing, 34
Moroccan chicken couscous, 47
Mushrooms: beef and mushroom
     burgers, 23
   mushroom and bacon risotto, 38
   pasta carbonara, 16
   steak, kidney and mushroom pie, 68
Mussels: Mediterranean fish stew, 78

Noodles with shrimp in lemon sauce, 15

Oatmeal and herb rack of lamb, 70
Onions: liver and onions, 33
Oranges: beef strips with orange and
   ginger, 27
Oxtail braised in red wine, 60

Parma ham: pork with Mozzarella and
   sage, 88
Parsley: country pork with a parsley
   crust, 43
Pasta: baked macaroni and cheese, 16
   baked pasta Bolognese, 51
   pasta carbonara, 16
   pasta with chicken livers, 92
   spaghetti with tuna sauce, 28
   tagliatelle with hazelnut pesto, 28
Peaches: glazed ham with spiced
   peaches, 71
Peking beef and pepper stir-fry, 82
Peppered steaks with Madeira, 85
Pies: Greek lamb pie, 40
   lamb pie with a potato crust, 50
   lamb, leek and apple pie, 58

ground beef pie with garlic potatoes,
     39
   steak, kidney and mushroom pie, 68
Plums: pork chops with plums, 62
Pork: Breton pork and bean casserole,
     84
   country pork with a parsley crust, 43
   ginger pork with black bean sauce, 86
   golden pork and apricot casserole, 52
   Louisiana rice, 46
   pork and celery popovers, 18
   pork roast in a blanket, 40
   pork steaks with gremolata, 91
   pork with Mozzarella and sage, 88
   pork chops with plums, 62
   pot-roast pork with celery, 67
   ruby pork chops, 94
   Texan barbecued ribs, 82
Potatoes: corned beef and egg hash, 26
   Cornish pasties, 19
   Irish stew, 65
   lamb pie with a potato crust, 50
   ground beef pie with garlic potatoes,
     39
Pumpkin: Jamaican bean stew, 94

Ragoût of veal, 36
Red currant-glazed lamb chops, 88
Rice: Chinese omelettes with fried rice,
     74
   kedgeree, 14
   Louisiana rice, 46
   mushroom and bacon risotto, 38
Rich beef casserole, 32
Roast beef with Yorkshire puddings, 64
Ruby pork chops, 94

Sage: pork with Mozzarella and sage, 88
Salmon with watercress sauce, 79
Sausages: Breton pork and bean
     casserole, 84
   sausage and bean ragoût, 48
   sausages and beans with dumplings, 35
   toad in the hole, 22
Shrimp: Chinese omelettes with fried
     rice, 74
   Mediterranean fish stew, 78
   noodles with shrimp in lemon sauce,
     15
Sizzling Chinese steamed fish, 74
Smoked haddock: kedgeree, 14
Sole with cider and cream, 76
Squid: Mediterranean fish stew, 78
Stir-fry: beef strips with orange and
     ginger, 27
   Peking beef and pepper stir-fry, 82

Texan barbecued ribs, 82
Toad in the hole, 22
Tomatoes: baked cod with tomatoes, 76
Trout: sizzling Chinese steamed fish, 74
Tuna: spaghetti with tuna sauce, 28
Turkish lamb and apricot stew, 42

Veal: ragoût of veal, 36

Watercress: salmon with watercress sauce, 79